Design in Embroidery

Early eighteenth-century embroidered picture made of satin worked in silk with long and short, split and satin stitches, with couched work (*V & A—crown copyright*).

Violet M. Endacott

Design in Embroidery

BONANZA BOOKS • NEW YORK

First published in the United States by
The Macmillan Company, MCMLXIV
Library of Congress catalog number 64—18410
© Violet M. Endacott MCMLXIII
Printed in the United States of America

This edition published by Bonanza Books,
a division of Crown Publishers, Inc.,
by arrangement with The Macmillan Co.,
a subsidiary of Crowell, Collier, and Macmillan, Inc.
b c d e f g h

Contents

Acknowledgments

The author wishes to thank Messrs. Edward Fairs and Wilfred Garnett for their care in taking photographs, and Mr. S. H. Glenister for his helpful advice and encouragement.

Grateful acknowledgment is also made to former students of Eastbourne Training College and Newland Park Training College, and to all owners of copyright material, for permission to reproduce their work. These sources are detailed beneath the illustrations. Designers and makers are indicated by the letters d and m.

The following additional abbreviations have been used:

CoID   Council of Industrial Design
DNM   Danish National Museum
EG   Embroiderers' Guild
ETC   Eastbourne Training College
FWI   Federation of Women's Institutes
GSA   Glasgow School of Art
NDS   Needlework Development Scheme
NPTC Newland Park Training College
RSM   Royal Scottish Museum
V & A   Victoria and Albert Museum

1 What to embroider

Like any form of embellishment, embroidery needs to be used with discrimination. A little fine work applied with thought and good taste can transform an ordinary article into something individual and exclusive. The decoration must, however, be considered as part of the article. The observer should not be impressed with the beauty of the embroidery, but rather with that of the table-cloth, or cushion, or blouse. Embroidery should never look as if it has been added as an afterthought. The function of the object to be embroidered should always be kept in mind too.

Having decided what to embroider, one must next choose the best fabric for the purpose. If the article will need frequent laundering, it should be of a suitably hard-wearing fabric. Real linen is expensive, but it is the best choice for the table. Some of the rayons, and wool and cotton mixtures, stand up to quite hard wear, and are obtainable in lovely shades. For a cushion, work bag or apron they could be used quite successfully.

A great deal of thought and planning is necessary before commencing work. Consideration of the type of embroidery, colour, threads, and stitchery are all vitally important.

Further advice on preliminary planning is given in Chapter 3 (pages 14 to 28).

Aprons In many countries aprons have for centuries been richly decorated, and frequently form a notable part of the national costume. Aprons of all types can be embellished with embroidery, but the purpose of the apron should always be kept in mind so that the design forms

Fig. 1.1 Apron of black-and-white half-inch check gingham, embroidered in white stranded cotton using fly and star stitches.

Fig. 1.2 Apron from white and blue lattice fabric, embroidered in blue stranded cotton (dm *Author*).

part of the whole garment. Check gingham is popular and lends itself to simple decoration. Smocking or pleating can be used to gather the fullness into the band and can be arranged to bring out one of the two colours of the check. The black-and-white check gingham apron shown in Fig. 1.1 was pleated at the top to bring out the black, the pleats being held in place by lines of fly stitch and stars worked in white thread. The waist-band was also pleated in the opposite direction and held in place by black fly stitches. At the bottom hem the fabric was pleated up to form the black-and-white stripes. Striped and spotted fabrics are also attractive for aprons, and lend themselves to decorative treatment (see Chapter 4).

A plain, thick cotton or linen crash can be used for gardening aprons and a little simple embroidery worked on a large pocket. A plain-coloured apron looks well with a pocket band and stitchery of a darker shade. Some very attractive aprons can be made from dark-coloured materials, embroidered in feather stitchery using several shades of embroidery thread. The Dorset feather stitchery has recently been revived, and is very suitable for this purpose. Fig. 1.2 shows an apron made from a white cotton lattice fabric. The lattice and double cross stitch embroidery are blue. The pocket is cut on the bias.

Dainty organdie aprons can make attractive gifts. These are best worked in shadow embroidery.

Lingerie can be given a personal look by a little well-chosen, well-worked embroidery. Pure silk is by far the best fabric for lingerie which is to be embroidered as it will wash and wear well. Decorative seams, faggoting, rouleaux, or decorative hems are effective. Appliqué, lace or net insets, or a little shadow embroidery can all look attractive. Designs should be small and dainty, and should appear to have been planned as part of the garment.

Blouses can be greatly improved by a little embroidery. Organdie, lawn, or silk blouses suit dainty tucks, rouleaux, or shadow embroidery, while linen blouses look well worked in drawn threadwork.

Collars, cuffs and belts can be gaily embroidered and used to brighten dark winter dresses. They should always be of a washable fabric (organdie or piqué is useful) and the design should suit the shape to be embroidered. Scalloped edges look effective. Collars and cuffs are best made to be detachable, so that they can be slipstitched into position. Avoid making accessories of this kind too conspicuous unless a marked contrast is deliberately intended.

Children's clothes lend themselves to decoration. Smocking is one of the most effective types of embroidery for small dresses. Fig. 1.3 shows one with smocking and a scalloped edge. Sometimes a little simple embroidery around the edge of the collar or at the bottom hem is appropriate. A dainty christening robe is a pleasure to make, and can be treasured and handed on from one generation to the next. Lawn, or very fine muslin, organdie or organza is suitable for this; small pin tucks can be pinstitched, and delicate touches of embroidery worked entirely in white. Children's playsuits can be decorated with appliqué, and very young children will be delighted to identify their own towels, face flannels or shoe bags by a small picture worked on each. Feeders should be made of linen or strong cotton which launders easily. They can be lined with plastic fabric (Fig. 1.4).

Wedding dresses and wedding veils are well worth embroidering. A very simple wedding dress can be enriched with embroidery, but if this is done great care is needed in selecting the style of the dress. A classic style

Fig. 1.4 Blue linen feeder, embroidered in white pulled work stitches (dm *K. Tipping*; *FWI*).

Fig. 1.3 White poplin child's dress embroidered in pink stranded cotton. Small eyelets and scalloping used for decoration (dm *J. Round, ETC*).

Fig. 1.5 Evening bag (*NDS*).

is suitable, with a fitted bodice, long sleeves fitting closely from elbow to wrist, and a long full skirt. Pure silk or very fine linen are ideal, but a more transparent fabric such as organdie or organza can be used. Embroider a design on the front panel of the dress, or try a border around the hem and running up the front, worked in white or cream with an occasional touch of silver or seed pearls, *but be very careful not to over-decorate*. If a metallic thread is to be used, choose Lurex as it will not tarnish. Wedding veils can be exquisitely embroidered. A spray should be worked in each of the three corners on one side of the net, and in the fourth on the other side, so that this corner can be worn thrown back from the head. The design is drawn on a piece of tracing paper or glazed cotton which is tacked to the net so that the design is visible through the mesh. It is then worked in chain stitch, or darning, and the tracing is removed when the work is finished. A border around the veil is effective; the net is cut to within $\frac{1}{4}$ in. of the embroidery. Nylon or silk net is the most suitable material to use. A small veil can be made from $1\frac{1}{2}$ yds of 54 in. net, and a full size veil from 2 yds of 72 in. net.

Embroidered toys, and decorative animals, birds, or insects are great fun to make and form attractive table decorations for a party. Scraps of material, beads, and sequins are all you will need; experiment with them and create your own designs. Decide on the characteristic features of the animal, bird, or creature you intend to make. Cut out the shapes as paper silhouettes and use these as patterns to cut from carefully chosen fabrics. Embroider these pieces before stitching them together, leaving a hole through which you can insert the stuffing. Close the hole, make the legs separately and try them in different positions before stitching them in place. The

Fig. 1.6 Embroidered felt toys (m
Jean Dickenson, ETC).

embroidery should emphasise the shape of the animal (Fig. 1.6). Children love doing this type of embroidery and can be allowed to make all sorts of fantastic creatures. Butterflies, fish, dragon-flies, beetles and birds are easy first attempts.

Bags of various types are suited to embroiderers at all levels. Work bags can be made in many different shapes and sizes, and almost any material and type of embroidery can be used. Fine work is needed for an evening bag, especially one made to match a particular dress. An attractive piece of material should be chosen, and beads, sequins and metallic threads can all be used. Fig. 1.5 shows an evening bag of black felt decorated with a bold design worked in red, different shades of blue and green stranded cotton, using sequins. Blanket, fly, detached wheatear, chain and twisted chain are the stitches used. The bag is lined with pink silk.

Beach bags are best made from a hard-wearing fabric such as sailcloth or linen, and they should be lined with plastic to make them waterproof. The one shown in Fig. 1.7 is of yellow linen embroidered with a sea-horse in various shades of green and black stranded cotton. The lining is green with yellow spots.

Pincushions are quick and easy to make and are thus suitable for beginners. They are useful for small or 'bazaar' gifts and are also a good way to try out any new kind of embroidery. Very little fabric is needed, and scraps can easily be used. Any shape or design can be chosen; the best stuffing to use is sawdust or bran. Handy for the dressmaker is a pincushion worn on the wrist on a piece of elastic. The one shown in Fig. 1.8 was made in patchwork using cuttings of Liberty silk. The diameter of each patch is only $\frac{1}{4}$ in. One side is turquoise and grey, and the reverse side yellow and turquoise.

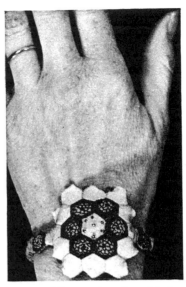

Fig. 1.8 Silk, patchwork, wrist pincushion in yellow and grey (dm *Author*).

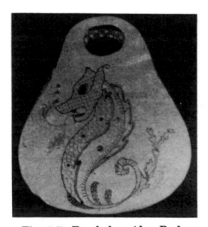

Fig. 1.7 Beach bag (dm *Barbara Smith, NPTC*).

Fig. 1.9a One way of placing decoration on table-mats. Another is shown in Fig. 1.9b.

Table and household linens are well worth embroidering. With careful choice of material they will wear for many years, and repay all the work that is put into them. Machine embroidery is very suitable for bed linen.

Table-cloths and napkins need frequent laundering, and should therefore be of good quality linen. The design for a table-cloth should be simple and dignified, and all the work should be as flat as possible, and so arranged that it will not be lost when the table is set for a meal. It is quite a good idea to lay the fabric on the table, arrange the cutlery and china, and mark with tailor's chalk the areas where the decoration will be most effective. Before choosing a design it is often helpful to consider the design of the china that is to be used on the cloth. Plain, line-banded and floral china all go well with drawn fabric stitches, but floral china should not be used with a cloth embroidered with different flowers. You can also make matching or contrasting table napkins with the same or a different motif in one corner.

Table-mats As for table-cloths, the best quality fabric should be chosen. It is helpful to place cutlery and china on the material before deciding the exact size and shape of the mats, and the positioning of the embroidery. A border decoration down each side of the mat, or decoration in the top-left hand corner is often suitable (Figs. 1.9a and b). Table-mats for use with hot plates can be made from a thick piece of cardboard backed with felt and covered with an easily laundered, embroidered, linen cover. These covers can be made double and the board slipped between the two pieces, or a piece of elastic which will grip the card can be sewn to the back of a single cover.

Sheets and pillowcases lend themselves to embroidery and this can also be a useful means of identifying them. A monogram, small spray or border pattern is suitable.

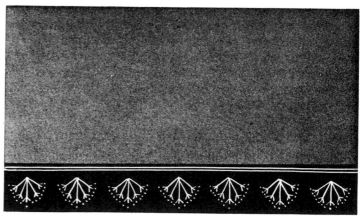

Fig. 1.9b

Embroidery should be placed centrally on or just below the top hem of a sheet. The decoration on pillowcases is best kept to the corners, or to one end, never in the centre where the head will rest. Babies' pillowcases in organdie with shadow embroidery are very attractive.

Hand towels are useful, especially as guest towels. A motif is usually worked on the thread with stitches such as cross stitch, or Assisi work, Hardanger, darning or geometric satin stitch. The decoration should not be too large, a small border at the bottom being most common. Never use too complicated a design for a towel. Plain hemstitching should be used for finishing the edges. Here too the embroidery can be used for identification, especially by children.

Tea-cosies These should be made to fit the pot. Ornate shapes are less efficient and should be avoided. Once again the design should fit the shape of the cosy. Suggestions are a small all-over pattern, a border running along the base, a stripe down the centre, or a central motif. Quilting is very appropriate as the thickness gives the warmth that is needed, and the embroidery is simple in design and execution. Tea-cosies should be carefully finished with a cord or piping. A hand-made cord is quickly made and looks effective. A dainty tea-cosy can be made from organdie embroidered with shadow work, and the edges finished with organdie points. Details of this finish are given in Chapter 32. For this type of cosy, a pad is made separately and can be quilted and placed loosely inside the organdie cover. The pad can be of a pale pastel shade to give a tinge of colour to the cosy. Fig. 1.10 shows a gay, white linen tea-cosy embroidered in blue, green, red and yellow threads.

Cushions are always welcome. They can be square, rectangular, triangular, circular, or of any suitable shape.

Fig. 1.11 Linen cocktail mat embroidered in cross stitch (dm *Author*).

Fig. 1.10 'Roundabout trio' tea-cosy (d *Margaret Bremner*, m *W. Douglass*; *CoID*).

Fig. 1.12 Wall hanging in appliqué work on a blue-grey satin background (dm *Author*).

Small cushions are now very fashionable and can give gay splashes of colour to a room. The design should always fit the shape and look well from any angle. Since the cushion will need to be cleaned or washed it is sensible to make the cover with a zip fastener opening. Fig. 1.13 shows a turquoise linen cushion embroidered in white threads, using various stitches to give different textures.

Curtains can sometimes be improved by a little simple embroidery, or a complementary pelmet can be made. Careful choice of fabric and colouring is essential. A bold simple design is best, as anything too complicated would take far too long to work and would look fussy. If the fabric is fairly heavy, use heavy threads such as tapestry wools or Anchor soft cotton. Couching, darning, buttonholing, or other composite stitches will give a good quick effect (Fig. 1.14). Always keep in mind that the work should be on a large scale. Light curtains can be made from muslin, scrim, organdie, or net. The design on these materials, which are transparent, will be visible in silhouette, so darning or drawn fabric stitches are effective. Machine embroidery can easily and suitably be used on organdie, organza or nylon.

Lampshades can be daintily embroidered. If thin linen scrim is worked in drawn fabric stitches the light will show up the pattern of holes. Organdie or nylon can also be embroidered with shadow work and then stitched over buckram. It is essential to remember that a lampshade must allow the light to come through; heavy fabrics are not suitable.

Screens and fire screens An old screen can be given new life if re-covered with some gay embroidery. Simple, cotton material such as gingham can be used, or a richer furnishing material. An interesting tweed with a pleasant texture or a furnishing satin would make a good back-

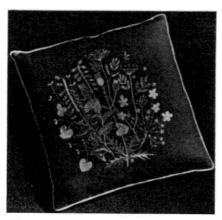

Fig. 1.13 'Wild flowers' cushion cover (d *Arthur Fairweather*, m *Miss L. Hay: CoID*).

ground. Appliqué or some other bold type of work is the most suitable embroidery.

Appliqué work or a simple design worked in various surface stitches is also effective for firescreens. Canvas work is occasionally used for these, but it is a very slow form of embroidery and the simpler patterns often look better.

Stool tops get hard wear, so a good linen should be used. Stools are fairly small, and canvas work is often appropriate.

Pictures and wall hangings are both popular and exciting. Any material can be used, and much of the interest should lie in the varying textures. As there are so many possibilities, further details are given in Chapters 3, 8 and 32. Both a picture and a hanging should have all the applied pieces going the same way as the background material. If this rule is not observed some of the pieces may stretch out of shape and pucker. When the work is finished it will need to be stretched and mounted. If a picture is to be covered with glass, it does not matter if some of the edges of material are unfinished, as they will not fray. Fig. 1.12 shows a wall hanging. The background is a rich blue-grey satin and the shapes are appliquéd on with various embroidery stitches.

Finger plates can be made from embroidered panel covered with glass or perspex. Figs 1.15 and 1.16 give patterns which could well be carried out in machine embroidery.

Decorative boxes make useful gifts. Jewel boxes can be of any shape and decorated with almost any kind of stitchery. First decide on the shape and size of your box, then cut out the pieces of card that you will need. Start with one for the base of the box and a similar one a fraction smaller for the lining of the base. The piece for

Fig. 1.15 Pattern for machine embroidery to be used on finger plates. Fig. 1.16 overleaf shows another.

Fig. 1.14 Heavy woollen curtain, decorated with a simple leaf pattern.

Fig. 1.16

the lid will be slightly larger than that for the base; the one to line the lid will be the same size as the base. Measure accurately the sides of the base, then cut a piece for each side of the box and a piece for each side of the lid which should be about $\frac{1}{2}$ in. deep. The lining of the sides of the box should be $\frac{1}{2}$ in. deeper than the outside, thus allowing for the lid to close. Very accurate measuring is essential in making any box. Embroider the pieces of fabric which should allow for $\frac{1}{2}$ in. turnings. Carefully place the base card on top of the fabric for the base, and use a colourless adhesive solution to paste down the $\frac{1}{2}$ in. turnings. Stretch these over the card cutting away extra fabric. Cover the other cards in the same way. A little wadding can be used to pad the lid or the lining of the lid or base. When all the pieces have been pressed, they are sewn together by oversewing, or overcasting in both directions. A small hand-made cord can be used to cover the joins, or a decorative embroidery stitch can be used. Fig. 1.17 shows a circular jewel box made from cream gros-grain. Silver thread was couched, and a little stitchery added with a fine blue silk thread. There is a blue embroidery stone in the centre, and a narrow piping of blue around the edge. The box is lined with deep blue tie silk which projects $\frac{1}{2}$ in. above the sides.

2 Tools and materials

Successful embroidery calls for use of the correct tools, though these are few in number. A good, small pair of scissors about 3 in. long with sharp points should be kept for embroidery and used for nothing else. A pair of cutting-out scissors will also be useful. A selection of needles is essential; a packet of assorted sizes will supply all that are needed. Crewel needles are the best for most types of embroidery. They are relatively short and have slender eyes, and although the eye-end is only slightly thicker than the point, they are comparatively strong. These needles are numbered to indicate the size, the higher the number the finer being the needle. Sizes No. 6, No. 8 and No. 10 will be sufficient for most kinds of work, though blunt tapestry needles are the best for some types of embroidery. The size of the needle is most important; it should pull through the material easily, and not make too large a hole. An embroidery frame is useful for certain pieces of work where the fabric needs to be held taut. The material should be fixed in the hoop or frame, at sufficient tension to keep the work from sagging or puckering when it is being worked.

Materials are as important as tools, and should always be very carefully considered. The fabric should be suitable for the purpose of the finished article, and the best quality should usually be chosen. It is always worth while spending a little extra on really good materials as these will give years of wear and pleasure. If the article is to be laundered, be sure the colour is fast, and that the fabric is shrink-resistant. If there is any doubt it is wise to wash the material before working it. It is a great

Fig. 1.17 Jewel box (dm *Author*).

disappointment to spend hours of work on an article which will not last for any length of time. The fabric needs to be carefully chosen to suit the type of embroidery to be worked on it. Linen scrim, even-weave Glenshee, or Glamis should be used for drawn threadwork and drawn fabric work. Looser, heavier types of even-weave materials should be used for cross stitch, double running, Holbein and Assisi work. Special Hardanger linen is available for Hardanger embroidery. Fine embroidery linen calls for delicate work with a thin thread and fine stitches. For contemporary work on pictures or hangings, all sorts of interesting fabrics are suitable.

If the article is to be square or rectangular, draw threads to make sure that the material is on the square. Tack all hems before beginning embroidery, or machine-neaten the fabric to prevent fraying. If the article is of a special shape, such as a tea-cosy or a circular cushion, cut a paper pattern, then tack around this to mark the shape on the fabric.

The threads used for embroidery should usually be in proportion to the thickness and weight of the background fabric. Too heavy or too thin a thread can spoil the finished effect. Stranded cottons, flosses and silks can be used for many forms of embroidery; most are available in six strands loosely twisted together. Varying thicknesses can be obtained by using a different number of these strands, which should be carefully separated. Pick off from the cut end the threads you want to use, hold them between the first finger and thumb of the right hand while holding the other threads between the third and fourth fingers. Take the entire strand of threads with the left hand, curling the fingers into the palm, inserting the thumb into the gap between the threads. Gently run the left thumb down to separate these threads. This will untwist them and prevent them from knotting with the uncurled fingers of the left hand.

The threads chosen should pull through the fabric easily. Use short lengths to prevent them becoming frayed or soiled. Beginners will be well advised to chose a smooth thread that does not knot, and to avoid types which are springy, or which tangle easily, as these are more difficult to work with. When the thread twists during working, hold it taut and run the needle right down to the face of the work. Grasp the thread between the right thumb and the first finger, and untwist it by drawing the nails along the length of thread. Twisting is often due to using a thread which is too long.

Begin work by making a few running stitches in the direction of the starting-point of the embroidery, then work over these stitches. To finish bring the thread through to the wrong side and make a small back stitch within the embroidery; carefully darn the needle through, cutting off the thread as near to the surface as possible. Avoid using knots or leaving loose ends on the wrong side of work.

A beginner will find it advisable to start with small articles that will be fairly quickly finished. Cottons, linens, and felt are more easily handled than slippery silks, satins or organdie.

If you are not familiar with the stitches you wish to use, practise them on a small piece of material. Learning embroidery stitches can be great fun if you make a sampler, creating your own pattern. Choose an interesting piece of material for the background, then cut a few simple shapes in newspaper. Use these as patterns to cut out from spare scraps of fabric. Arrange the fabric shapes on the background in a pleasing pattern and tack each piece in place. Work the various embroidery stitches to

Fig. 2.1 Experimental sampler of stitches and fabrics.

Fig. 3.1 Motifs based on the snow-flake pattern.

complete the effect. Fig. 2.1 was worked in this way. A piece of cream grosgrain was used as a background and pieces of turquoise and of deep peacock fabric were appliquéd before various stitches were added.

3 Designing

The word 'design' is difficult to define, but it implies a plan or a sense of order. To design is not simply to apply ornament or decoration, but rather to ensure that the finished article is a unity in which the individual features are subservient to the whole. The problem in designing a pattern for embroidery is how best to fill a given space, whether it is with a single pattern, the units of a repeating pattern or a motif. But the word 'fill' must not be taken literally; the unembroidered areas are part of the design, and it should always be remembered that space is as important as decoration.

In selecting a pattern, whether it is to stand by itself, to be repeated or to be linked to others, we have the world around us as a source of inspiration. The natural world in particular is full of pattern. Think, for example, of the formation of a snowflake or crystal (see Fig. 3.1).

Some basic principles
The fundamentals of design are timeless and apply to all crafts, though different aspects of them have been stressed at different times. The first principle is unity: no part of

the finished article should obtrude. Closely related to this is harmony: every line or shape must blend with the rest. We can see both these qualities in nature in, for example, the form of a beautiful animal. In the natural world unrelated shapes are usually the result of some disaster. One has only to think of the shape of a tree before and after it has been struck by lightning to see that this is so.

Proportion is of equal importance. Taken together the various parts of a whole should complement and not compete with one another. The total effect should be one of balance.

This is not to say, however, that contrast has no place in a good design. The correct use of contrast, whether it be of size, line, shape, colour, tone or texture, gives liveliness and variation. This can be seen in Fig. 3.2. Learn to distinguish between simplicity and monotony, and avoid a laboured or confused effect, especially when planning an intricate design or one which calls for skilled craftsmanship in execution.

Every good design will have a focal point, or centre of interest. This can be achieved by the use of colour, size, or shape, but there should never be more than one dominant feature. Some patterns, however, consist of a repeated series of individual patterns, each having its own focal point.

An object can be said to be well designed only if it is suited to its purpose. Shape, size and materials must be functional and ornament used only when it is not an encumbrance. Decoration planned for one space may be quite wrong when used in a different place, or shape. Each material has its own limitations, and these too control the choice of design.

The only way to learn to design is, bearing these basic

Fig. 3.2 Mid-seventeenth-century wool embroidery in monochrome (dark blue-green) on linen and cotton material, designed for use as a curtain (*V & A—crown copyright*).

principles in mind, to observe and to experiment. Some practical hints may, however, be useful.

Special problems in designing for embroidery

In designing buildings, furniture or pottery, there are three dimensions—height, width and depth—to be considered; but in embroidery only length and width need be borne in mind, as the background is flat. It is therefore best to ignore perspective and depth. In designing with natural forms such as flowers, leaves, animals or figures, do not attempt to show recession (i.e. to depict them 'in the round'). The design should be entirely flat, but spaced so as to give a pleasing arrangement of shapes.

As has already been stressed, it is essential to remember the conditions under which the piece of work will be seen. A wall hanging, for example, needs a bold and striking design built round the correct combination of lines and shapes; fine stitchery is wasted. Objects to be seen at close quarters, on the other hand, can have delicate stitchery with fine fillings and interesting details.

It is profitable to study the pieces of embroidery displayed in museums and make a careful analysis of the design used in them. Find how areas are divided into different shapes, and what fillings are used in each of these spaces. The Syon Cope, for example, is wonderfully designed and so are some of the other large copes which are divided into architectural shapes. Notice that if lettering was used at all it was an integral part of the design; for example, the name of a saint might be worked in his halo or on a scroll in his hand. Fig. 3.3 shows an all-over design that will repay study. Some of the Elizabethan embroideries show beautiful repeating patterns, especially some of those done in blackwork. Small units from these can be adapted for modern work. It will be seen that some

Fig. 3.3 Part of a linen jacket, with yellow silk embroidery, made in England in the late seventeenth or early eighteenth century (*V & A—crown copyright*).

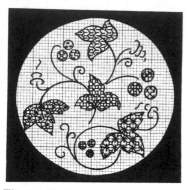

Fig. 3.4 Design for a circle.

Fig. 3.5

of the work of the late sixteenth and early seventeenth centuries is poor in design. The motifs lack coherent arrangement, and it is probable that they were taken haphazardly from herbals and embroidery pattern books. This lack of care in the arrangement of motifs was, however, sometimes compensated by careful choice of colour or of stitchery, which gave a certain unity to the whole. Some of the units themselves are very beautiful and can with careful arrangement be used today.

Your aim should be to make a decoration in embroidery that could not be made in any other medium. This involves in particular an imaginative use of textures and colour. To make the most of these you should concentrate on achieving a flowing design, full shapes and an appropriate choice of stitches.

Get to know the possibilities of various threads, of the needle as a tool, of different fabrics as backgrounds. Discover all the different fabrics available for embroidery; the shops have a wonderful selection that will lend themselves to simple designs. Save all the scraps from dressmaking, as they can often be an inspiration.

Planning the design

Think carefully before beginning any piece of work. Decide what you are going to make, what size and shape it is to be, and the position and size of the decoration. Consider the fabric to be used; bearing in mind its colour and texture, and the way these can be used to carry out the design you have in mind. The pattern must fit not only the shape, but also the material; certain backgrounds suggest specific types of embroidery. Always design for a particular shape (for example, a rectangular border, a triangular corner, a circle (Fig. 3.4), a square) and avoid 'bitty' patterns. Plan your work in advance. If, for

Fig. 3.6

example, a join is necessary in a large piece of work, consider the placing of the seam, and make it part of the design, or arrange the design so that it is concealed. In a bedspread two seams down the sides will probably be better than a central seam. Next seek inspiration for the pattern. Geometric ideas can be worked out on squared paper, or simple abstract shapes can be grouped in interesting ways, the effect of which is due not only to the contrasting shapes but also to the contrasts of texture, tone and colour.

It is often helpful to begin by experimenting with simple paper cuts. Take a circle or a square, fold it several times, then cut shapes out of it. This will give a simple symmetrical silhouette that can be used as a basis for embroidery. (Figs. 3.5 and 3.6 show examples.)

Next try border patterns. Cut simple units (e.g. leaf shapes) and repeat them, linking with a line, as shown in Fig. 3.8. Other symmetrical patterns can be made by folding a piece of paper down the middle and then cutting out a shape, as in Fig. 3.7. The effectiveness of a border may depend not only on the motifs but also on the spaces between them.

Working with paper cuts has the advantage that you are dealing with shapes rather than lines. Characteristic silhouettes of animals or birds can be cut in paper. Just a plain side or front view is best, simplified so that the shape is typical of the creature. Appliqué and inlay should always be designed in this way. Designs can also be built up by tacking around a paper cut-out, then outlining with embroidery stitches, and developing the detail with further stitchery. Think from the beginning of your materials and choice of stitches and you will avoid being forced to modify your design half-way through.

Designing direct on to material is another method which

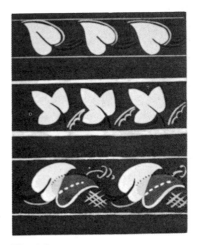

Fig. 3.8

Fig. 3.7

Fig. 3.9 Cross stitch border designs drawn on graph paper.

can be used. A good, simple beginning is to build the pattern on the threads by counting. Some articles can be designed in this way without any drawn or written plan. This form of designing is especially suitable for pulled work, borders and motifs being built up by combining various stitches and fillings. Designs for surface embroidery can also be made direct on the fabric; various combinations of stitches being used with variation in thickness of thread and colour. These motifs may often grow outwards from the centre, which remains the focal point. Sometimes it is best to experiment on a separate piece of fabric before beginning the actual work, but it is important that this trial sample should be of the same size, as a change of scale can entirely alter the effect. Another way of designing without a drawn or written plan is when patterned or textured fabrics are used as a background. In Chapter 4 designing with checks, stripes and spots is discussed, but other patterned or textured fabrics can be used and stitches combined to form patterns, or to elaborate existing patterns. Stitches are often worked in one or other of the colours to alter the balance and proportion between background and pattern. Another possibility is to use fresh colour to add interest. Stitches, braids, beads or sequins can be used in this way.

In cross stitch, Assisi work, Holbein, double running and blackwork, patterns can be worked out on graph paper, then worked directly on to the fabric by counting the threads (Fig. 3.9).

When more planning is necessary, make a drawing, carefully positioning the decoration in relation to the whole object. Proportion is always most important, both of the object itself, and of the decoration in relation to the object. Remember, however, that a drawing made in pencil may be quite unsuitable for carrying out in stitchery. As much designing as possible should always be done directly on the material by the skilful use of stitchery. A few guide lines can be drawn, then fillings and details of finer stitchery can be worked freely to give the texture. It is important to plan a design in the scale in which it will be carried out. Some designs can be enlarged or reduced but if this is done some sort of modification is usually necessary.

Developing a sense of design

Study shapes, in an endeavour to acquire the power of discriminating between good and bad. A shape is good if it possesses qualities of harmony, rhythm and proportion. Sensitivity to line and form may be cultivated by observing these characteristics in nature, where two things are seldom identical and where there is order without tedium. An ordered regularity in design can be pleasing, but hand and eye give a pleasant irregularity which will not come if ruler and compasses are used. Cut out simple and interesting shapes in paper or fabric, and move these about until you find a pleasing arrangement. Experiment with pins, fabric shapes and rug wool on a fabric background (the rug wool represents the lines). Try arranging them in as many different ways as possible, until you get a satisfying result; selecting the shapes that look well together and discarding those that do not fit in so well.

It will also be noticed that the relation of shapes to one another is most important. A pattern with shapes of equal size can be dull and uninteresting, but shapes of too widely different sizes can be discordant. Shapes should on the whole be full and rounded, and small angles should be avoided as these give a restless effect.

Experiment next with line (Figs. **3.10a** and *b*). Lines

Fig. 3.10b Designs using line.

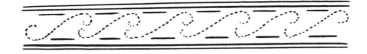

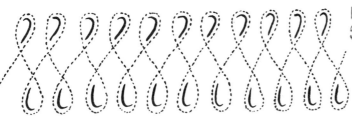

Fig. 3.10a Designs using line.

Fig. 3.11 Simple counter-change.

Fig. 3.12

give rhythm, direction and vitality to any piece of work, as well as linking the more solid shapes. The designer needs to be familiar with the various line stitches, as each gives a different quality of line. Whipped running gives a different effect from couching, Pekinese, chain, or herring-bone stitch. Choose your stitch according to whether you require a light, heavy, broken or wavy line.

In any design, gradation of tone is important, as tone contrasts bring interest to the work and emphasise some shapes more than others. If you want to test your work for tone contrast, look at it through half-closed eyes. The best way to study tone is to experiment. First, try counter-change (Fig. 3.11). Only rarely is counter-change used in its pure form (that is when each part is matched by one identical in size and shape but of a contrasting tone value), but the principle of contrasting tone values is useful to keep in mind. Continue by cutting out two shapes, one straight-sided, and the other curved, one in black and one in white. Arrange these two shapes in different ways until a satisfactory pattern is formed. Now experiment, as in Fig. 3.12, with three pieces of paper, black, white and grey, each of a simple shape. In nature we see simple silhouette shapes (e.g. leaves, trees or plants) and these may provide ideas (Figs. 3.13a and b).

Texture

Texture is always important in design. Notice textures in everyday things—in the weave of fabric, the grain of wood, the uneven surface of brick or concrete, a field of corn, frog's spawn, a bird's egg, fur on the cat's back, a snail's shell, seaweed, shells, sand on the sea-shore, the bark of a tree, the veins of a leaf, and grain in marble or tiny pebbles. In embroidery, texture is a valuable quality,

Fig. 3.13a

for it can impart an interest and beauty distinct from that arising from colour. Indeed, work done entirely in white or natural threads is wholly dependent on the variations in tones arising from the use of various textures.

Every piece of work is made more interesting if the texture varies between rough and smooth, and if some of the pattern is filled in to give a solid effect in contrast to the web of lines. Contrasts in textures are important, too, in relation to the use of the finished article. A rough tweed upholstery on a chair may, for example, call for a smooth, shiny-surfaced cushion.

Changes in texture can be achieved by careful choice of stitches, background fabric and threads, and by altering the direction of stitches (a device which, as is pointed out below, often has an effect on tone also). Experiment with various threads and stitches, and you will discover the particular characteristics of each. Threads can, for example, be thick or fine, dull or shiny. Varying the thickness of thread can be most effective, but remember that a thread must be chosen in relation to its background fabric. Do not use too heavy a thread on a fine fabric, and vice versa. Fig. 3.14 shows the central design of a table-cloth embroidered with threads of varying thickness; these, and the different stitches, provide texture interest. A medium weight fabric will often give an opportunity to use a variety of thicknesses in this way. Part of a smooth background fabric can be worked to give the illusion of roughness, while a loosely woven fabric can in parts be given a smooth texture. Some stitches, such as satin stitch, long and short stitch, or closely worked stem stitch, will give a smooth appearance. Others, such as buttonhole stitch, fly stitch, Roumanian or feather stitch, give a rougher effect. A shiny thread can be used for emphasis in an otherwise dull-textured embroidery.

Fig. 3.14 Detail from a coral linen table-cloth embroidered in white *coton-à-broder*, Anchor Soft and varying thicknesses of stranded cottons. The stitches used are chain, stem, thorn, coral, feather, rosette, buttonhole, French knots and herringbone (dm *Doreen Wood, ETC*).

Fig. 3.13b

Fig. 3.15 Flat areas of colour broken up by texture.

Altering the direction of stitches can be used to help obtain variety of tone value, especially in embroidery of only one colour; the light catches the stitchery at different angles. Radiating stitches sometimes provide an interesting contrast to vertical or horizontal stitches. Direction of stitch is of course also important in suggesting growth, and giving vitality to a piece of work. Variety can also be achieved by breaking up the work with various fillings, each of which will give a different effect. Lacy drawn fabric stitches or darning fillings can add richness, in contrast to more solid mass fillings. Superimposing one fabric on top of another will also focus the attention.

The importance of colour

Finally, there is the question of colour. This is a powerful agent for good or ill; its proper use, or its misuse, can make or mar a piece of work.

Many theories of colour have been put forward, but most people's colour sense develops best from experiment, and from their own natural enjoyment. The appreciation of colour is a very personal thing, but it is nevertheless worth while striving to develop and extend one's powers of discrimination, while guarding always against prejudice about particular combinations. Observation from nature is again invaluable. Notice, for example, the leaves in autumn, butterflies' wings, the feathers of a bird, and the wonderful tints of the sky and sea. You will soon appreciate that in nature there are very few pure colours, and these are used sparingly, in splashes on flowers and fruits. Most colours are half-tones, or neutrals. Even shadows on the most brilliant flowers are a blend of neutral tones. Notice the different qualities of grey—it can be cool, warm, light or strong. To appreciate this wide range, collect from scraps of paper, fabrics, stamps, etc., as many different shades of one colour as you can.

There are seven main hues, red, orange, yellow, green, blue, indigo and violet. Together they comprise the colour circle, yellow being the lightest, and blue the darkest. Those which come opposite each other on the circle, e.g. red and green, blue and yellow, orange and blue-green, are contrasts. Tones are made by adding black to the hues and tints by adding white.

Colour in its most brilliant, pure form, will dominate a pattern, and needs to be softened with some more sombre shades. If pale colours or tints are to predominate, a touch of a bright colour or of white will give life to the pattern. White or black embroidery is effective on a tinted background. For example, white is pleasing on blue or coral, while black on yellow or lime gives good contrast.

When any colour is placed with a contrasting one it will appear brighter, but two or more colours should not usually be used in equal quantities. A pattern all in pale tints looks lifeless, but one with several dominant hues appears garish. A good scheme can be built up using only one basic colour with several of its own tones and tints; such a monochrome treatment can be most effective in embroidery. Sometimes a splash of brilliant colour will enliven a combination of neutrals. Large flat areas of colour can be broken up by changes in texture or by different stitchery fillings. Gradation of colour can be useful and can be combined with broken or flat effects obtained by powdered fillings, or shaded satin, or long and short stitch (see Fig. 3.15). Never try to use colour in slavish imitation of nature; it is always better to be imaginative and venturesome.

The balance between lines and masses, and solid areas and lighter ones, also has to be considered. If an article

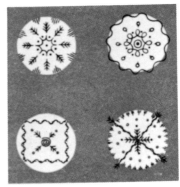

Fig. 3.16 Patterns based on a circle.

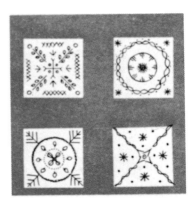

Fig. 3.17 Patterns based on a square.

Fig. 3.18

Fig. 3.19a Early eighteenth-century wool embroidery on cotton and linen, using satin and stem stitches with speckling, in dull rose and pink (*V & A—crown copyright*).

Fig. 3.19b Early eighteenth-century wool embroidery on cotton and linen, using satin, stem and buttonhole stitches with speckling in dull rose and pink (*V & A—crown copyright*).

is to be viewed as a picture or hanging, the weight (that is, the darker shades or more solid masses) should be slightly towards the bottom, otherwise the work is likely to look top-heavy. The placing of accent is extremely important, for the tone of the whole design is set by the central point of interest. Decide what you want to emphasise in your pattern, and how best to achieve this. Striking patches of primary colour, carefully considered in relation to the whole colour scheme, are useful, or strong tone contrasts when only one hue is being used.

When deciding the colour scheme of a particular piece of work, consider its purpose. If it is to be the focal point of interest in a room any colours may be used, but if it is intended to blend with an existing scheme it must fit in unobtrusively. No one piece of household embroidery should be too individual or assertive, as it may be out of place in relation to the rest of the furnishings in the room.

Avoid restlessness in any colour scheme that embraces more than one article. Bright strong tones may be used only if they are considered in relation to the existing colours.

All these remarks, however, are only pointers—suggestions as to how one's artistic sense (or taste) may be educated and brought to bear on questions of colour. How important taste is can be seen from some of the beautiful peasant work which uses combinations that are unusual, even daring—and completely successful.

Form

The simplest designs in embroidery are often the best. A few very simple motifs and lines can be used in an infinite number of patterns (Figs. 3.16 and 3.17). Experiment with them, to produce variations and developments which will form your own designs.

Fig. 3.20

Plants should be given a decorative and abstract rather than a naturalistic treatment. It is best to design with plants only after you have done quite a lot of experimenting with stitchery and abstract patterns. At first try to think of the characteristics of all flowers, rather than those of any particular flower. Draw plants in various scales but conventionalise them and treat them in a formalised way. Notice, for example, the simple, convex, rounded shapes that are so pleasing an aspect of many plants. Grasses, ferns and fruits, as well as leaves and flowers, can be treated in this way. Patterns based on a section through a fruit are shown in Fig. 3.18.

When designing from plant forms, draw the main stems first, remembering the direction of growth, and being careful not to have any lines crossing at right angles. The stems should flow freely, but should not run directly to any corner of the shape being filled. Next draw the outline of the leaves and flowers, partly covering the main stems (Fig. 3.20).

There is an infinite variety of simple flower and leaf shapes, the outline of which can be used in pattern making. Figs. 3.19a and b give examples. Collect different shaped leaves and flowers, dry and press them, then make as many different arrangements with them as you can. Cut out simple leaf shapes in paper and see how easy it is to create a design by adding a few simple brush strokes (Fig. 3.21).

Birds, animals, insects, butterflies, and fish also have interesting silhouettes and a good beginning can be made by cutting out the simple shape of each in paper. Give unity to the chosen design with a few lines (Figs. 3.22 and 3.23). The human form can be treated in a similar way, and has often been used in peasant embroideries. Look through a microscope at the section of a fruit or a flower,

Fig. 3.22a

Fig. 3.22b

Fig. 3.21

Fig. 3.23

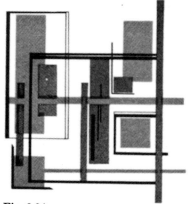

Fig. 3.24

at a snowflake, a crystal or a butterfly wing and you will find inspiration for many embroideries.

Experiment, especially with line and texture, and never make your design too realistic. Do not copy slavishly from a book although reference to good nature books can be useful. Photographic representation is not wanted; shapes should be used symbolically. It does not matter if the object is not immediately recognisable, provided that interest is given by the individual shapes and the way they are grouped. It is best to take only your ideas from objects and natural forms around you, and to allow your treatment of them to be quite fanciful. Each person will interpret the forms in a differen   vay, for the art of design is essentially individual.

Church brasses, wrought-iron gates, man-hole covers, book jackets, wrappings on cosmetics, pottery, and household furniture, as well as buildings, can all be adapted as ideas for design.

In many forms of embroidery geometric designs are suitable. Patterns for quilting are, for example, almost always of this type, and simple household objects such as cups, plates and saucers are frequently used by the designer. Circles, squares, rectangles and triangles can all be used, either separately or combined in one pattern (Fig. 3.24). Many cross-stitch designs are also built up on geometric shapes (Fig. 3.9). Tiles, mosaics and Roman pavements are useful examples.

4 Designing with gingham, checks, spots and stripes

Checks

Even checked material provides a good base for interesting and quite elaborate patterns. The most effective use of check gingham is to block out one of the coloured checks with the other colour, e.g. red-and-white check with red embroidery on the white squares and white embroidery on the red squares.

Large check gingham is perhaps the easiest to start with, as small patterns can be worked in some of the squares. Black-and-white gingham has the most striking effect. Lines can be worked diagonally, joining the corners of the squares, or spots, stars, or circles can be embroidered in some of them. These large checks can also be easily pleated to form a band of colour. Press the pleats with an iron, being sure the fold is exactly on the line of colour. Tack the pleats down to keep them in position, then embroider to keep them in place. Fly stitch can be used; lines of chain stitch, herringbone, chevron, stem or back stitch are good for this type of embroidery (Fig. 1.1). Bands of pleating can also be used at the bottom of a skirt or apron, as well as at the waist to dispose of the fullness, but care must always be taken in the placing of these bands to see that the proportions are right. If the band is too wide it may look heavy, or if it is too near the bottom of the garment it may look as if the decoration is dropping down. Bands of bias or coloured tape can be used to block out a row of squares. These bands should be fixed down with embroidery stitches—whipped running, fly stitch, lazy daisy or variations of blanket stitch.

Smaller check gingham with ¼ in. squares is also suitable

Fig. 4.2 Red and white check gingham apron, decorated with a bias strip of gingham in a larger check. The smocking and embroidery are in red stranded cotton (dm *Hazel Bower, ETC*).

Fig. 4.3 Child's dress made in brown and white check gingham, embroidered with white cross stitch and ric-rac. The white organdie collar is whipped with a brown thread (dm *Author*).

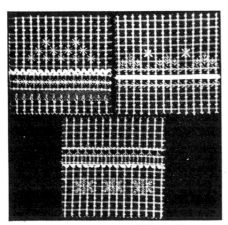

Fig. 4.1 Experiments with seerloop gingham.

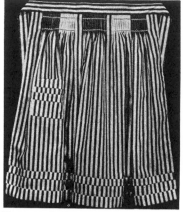

Fig. 4.4 Coffee and cream striped apron, the decoration of which has been achieved by careful cutting and seaming (dm **K. E. Honey, ETC**).

Fig. 4.5 Child's dress made in blue and grey striped cotton. The embroidery on the pale blue organdie collar is in a slightly deeper shade of blue. Fullness is gathered into bands of pleats which are fixed with lines of close herringbone and dots of chain stitch (dm **Author**).

for pleating and for decorating with bands of embroidery. Ric-rac can be effectively used on this material, couched on with a coloured thread, or placed beneath a pleat so that only the points are visible. Fig. 4.1 shows experiments with seerloop gingham.

Very small check gingham lends itself to cross-stitch decoration, in which one colour is blocked out with thread of the other. Experiment with various patterns. A bias strip of large squared gingham may be applied to a smaller check material (Fig. 4.2). Cut the bias strips so that a complete square shows, allowing for a ¼ in. turning each side. Fig. 4.3 shows decoration on a child's dress; cross stitch and ric-rac were used.

Striped material

This also lends itself to pleating, and to bands applied with the stripes going the opposite way. Bias binding, coloured tapes, or ric-rac can also be used. Lines of embroidery can be worked between the stripes, or if the stripes are wide enough the embroidery can be on the stripe, as in Fig. 4.6. Small articles can be given interest by seaming pieces together with stripes going in different directions, but great accuracy is needed to be sure the stripes match exactly. Chevrons and various square mosaic patterns can also be formed by careful arrangement. Fig. 4.4 shows a striped apron that has been pleated at the top to form bands of colour. The decoration on the pocket and at the bottom hem has been achieved by cutting the fabric in strips and seaming it so that the stripes alternate. In Fig. 4.5 is a child's dress decorated at the hem with a stripe of bias binding fastened with fly stitch. The fullness is pleated into the yoke to form bands of colour which are fastened down with rows of herringbone, and small spots of chain stitch. The spots are

Fig. 4.6 Decoration for a half-inch stripe fabric.

repeated on the organdie collar which is edged with buttonhole stitch. Fig. 4.7 suggests the use of a striped fabric in making a cushion.

Striped aprons can well be finished with a pointed edge and plain facing. Cut a facing 3 in. wide and tack it to the material with the right sides together. With pencil and ruler draw dots $\frac{1}{2}$ in. from the raw edges, and about 1 to $1\frac{1}{2}$ in. apart. Next draw another row of dots, 1 in. above the previous row and alternating with them. Join these dots to make a zigzag line. Carefully machine along this zigzag line, turning at the points with the machine needle down. Trim off the turnings to within $\frac{1}{8}$ in., snipping carefully at the points. Turn the facing to the wrong side, then press it and turn it up level with the base of the points. Turn in the raw edges on the wrong side and slipstitch in place. No stitching should show on the right side of the garment (Fig. 4.8).

Spotted materials

This material may be improved by simple decoration—for example, spots can be embroidered with circles, or with stitches radiating from them, zigzag or curved lines can be worked between certain spots. Couching is useful for linking or making a scroll pattern around some of the spots. A line of spots may be formed by pleating. Pointed or scalloped edges, such as those shown in Fig. 4.9a and b are most effective. To make the scallops, place a strip of plain or striped cotton fabric 3 in. wide on top of the spotted material, with the right sides facing, and tack the two pieces together. Make a cardboard template using a penny, halfpenny, or a pair of compasses. Using this template, draw scallops so that a spot is in the centre of each. Machine on the line, turning sharply at each point with the needle down. Trim off the edges to within

Fig. 4.8 Striped green and white apron with a decorative pocket, finished with a pointed edge and a green facing (dm *S. Hallam, ETC*).

Fig. 4.9a Decoration of spotted fabric with a scalloped edge.

Fig. 4.9b Decoration of spotted fabric with a pointed edge.

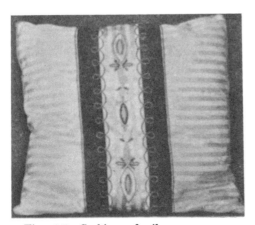

Fig. 4.7 Cushion of silver-grey striped rayon. The stripes run vertically on central panel. Wine ribbon covers the seams (dm *Author*).

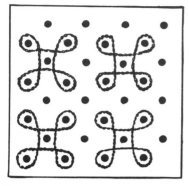

Fig. 4.10 Spots linked with a scroll of chain stitch.

Fig. 4.11 Fly stitch and herringbone used as links on a spotted fabric.

$\frac{1}{8}$ in. of the machine line. Carefully snip up to each point. Turn the facing up to the wrong side and fold it down so that it just touches the bottom of the scallops, then fold it up again to the top of the scallops on the wrong side. Turn under a small hem and slipstitch in place. Figs. 4.10 to 4.13 suggest other ways of using spots.

5 Enlarging a design

The original design should be squared up with faint pencil lines $\frac{1}{2}$ in. apart. If the design is in a book or if it is not possible to draw over it, trace it first. Next draw on a piece of paper the same number of squares, proportionately larger according to the size of the new design. The pattern is then copied piece by piece into the squares. Patterns can be reduced in a similar way, by drawing squares smaller than those on the original design. See Figs. 5.1a and b.

A different method may be used if the design is difficult to square up. Enclose the design in a rectangle, draw the diagonal across this rectangle, then with set-square and ruler draw another, larger rectangle with a diagonal parallel to the first. This rectangle will be in proportion to the first. Now draw the other diagonal on each of the rectangles and then the vertical and horizontal lines through the point where these cross. This gives four smaller rectangles with one diagonal in each. Draw the other diagonal and the horizontal and vertical lines as for

Fig. 4.12 Fly, lazy daisy and stroke stitches used to form a pattern on a spotted fabric.

the larger rectangles. The design can now be easily copied (Fig. 5.2).

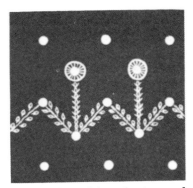

Fig. 4.13 Lazy daisy, wheatear, and blanket stitches used to form a border pattern on a spotted fabric.

6 Transferring designs to the fabric

There are several different ways of transferring a design to fabric.

Wax transfer paper is the simplest method, and can be used with any smooth fabric such as cotton, silk or linen. Transfer paper is obtainable in several colours. Place the paper gently on the fabric, then the design on top of that. Pin the three layers together, being careful not to move the transfer or smudge the fabric. Go over the design with a hard pencil or stylo, and the markings will be transferred to the fabric. Afterwards remove the papers with care.

Tracing can be used for transparent fabrics such as organdie or fine silk, which should be placed directly over the design. This is then outlined on to the fabric with a very thin paint prush and a touch of watercolour paint.

Pouncing is one of the most useful methods. Trace the design on tracing paper. Place this paper on a soft pad, and prick along all the lines with a thick pin, being sure you go right through the paper each time. Keep the holes close together. A tracing wheel can be used for long lines. Next pin the pricked design over the material which is to receive it. Dip the end of a small roll of soft cloth in french chalk for dark material, or charcoal for light

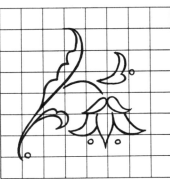

Fig. 5.1b

Fig. 5.1a

Fig. 5.2

material. Rub this well over the pricked design so that it penetrates the holes. When the entire design has been covered in this way, remove the tracing, being very careful not to smudge the outline. Now, using a very fine paint brush, and watercolour, paint over these lines. When this is dry, flick off the chalk or charcoal with a piece of cotton fabric.

For woollen materials, and those with a rough surface, cut out the various shapes of the pattern in paper, then tack around them. Remove the paper shapes, and draw in the main lines with tailor's chalk.

Another method is to trace the design on thin tissue-paper, then tack this to the material. Outline the design with large running stitches, before tearing away the tissue paper.

'*Aquarell*' *pencils* are very useful for drawing directly on fabric. These pencils are obtainable in twelve colours and wash out quite easily.

Special transfer ink is also obtainable, or can be made from a solution of sugar (a tablespoonful of sugar dissolved in half a tea-cup of boiling water) coloured with some blue from the blue-bag. This ink is used to outline the design on a piece of paper. When it is dry the paper is placed face-down on the material and ironed with a hot iron. This causes the design to be transferred to the material.

7 Assisi work

Assisi is everywhere famous as the small town in Italy where Francis Bernardone was born and is buried. Saint Francis, founder of the religious order of Franciscans, is known by the local people as *Poverello*. For centuries, sisters of the convents of Assisi divided their time between prayer and work, producing some exquisite pieces of linen embroidery for use in the churches. In the thirteenth and fourteenth centuries, beautiful embroideries were worked, and many of them have been preserved in Italian churches and museums. Animal motifs were used, simply designed and outlined, the background of the pattern being filled in with very fine cross stitch. St Francis' love of animals and birds inspired these early designers, and much of their work bears motifs and characters taken from episodes in his life, resembling in this the frescoes and murals of Giotto. In later years peasants began doing similar embroideries for their homes, and finding they could earn a little money from selling these, they practised until they became extremely skilled.

At the beginning of this century the women of Assisi revived this type of work, and today, tourists find it has become a local cottage industry. At first designs were copied from old embroideries; later, patterns were inspired by the wood carvings on stalls, chairs and chests in the churches. The patterns in Fig. 7.1 are similar to the beautiful carvings of the dome of San Rufino at Assisi, and of the church of San Pietro at Perugia. In recent years the work has spread from Assisi all over the world. Genuine Assisi work can however usually be distinguished

Fig. 7.1 Patterns for Assisi embroidery.

Fig. 7.2 Border of a linen table-runner embroidered in Assisi work. The background is cream, and the outline of the design is worked in black, with light green cross-stitch background (m *Margery Ray, ETC*).

by the fact that in one corner is embroidered a small cross, or the heraldic badge of the town consisting of a lion rampant beside a cross.

Cushions, chair-backs, table-runners, tray-cloths or table-cloths can be decorated with this type of embroidery, which is a good one for beginners to design.

Designs are usually heraldic in character and can be drawn on graph paper. Birds and beasts are outlined, then the crosses for the background are worked by counting the threads. The material used is usually white, cream or natural, and the warp and weft threads need to be of the same thickness. The outline stitch is double running or back stitch, and is worked in a dark thread—black, navy, nigger brown or very dark green. The cross stitch background is a lighter, brighter colour, rust, scarlet, jade and china blue being popular. A soft, china blue background with navy blue outlining is effective, and gives something of the antique effect of the old Assisi embroideries.

Borders are usually worked in a mixture of cross stitch and Holbein stitch. Both stitches should be worked in two journeys. For the outlining, start by making each stitch and space equal, then come back along the same line filling up the gaps left in the first journey. The line of the second journey can be kept straight by inserting the needle above the stitch made in the first journey and bringing it out below the other end of the stitch. All outlines should be worked first.

The cross stitch background should also be worked in two journeys, taking care that all the top threads of the crosses lie in the same direction so that the effect will be even. A border of Holbein stitch is usually used to soften the hard outline of the panel of embroidery. This helps to make the pattern merge better into the material. Fig. 7.2

Fig. 7.3 Chair-back embroidered with a wide border of Assisi work, a narrow border of Holbein stitch, and a hem-stitched edge.

shows a border of black Holbein stitch, then another small border of green cross stitch matching the cross stitch of the background.

The old Italian embroiderers used two-sided cross stitch for Assisi work. With this method, if the work is carefully done, it is almost impossible to tell which is the wrong side.

Articles embroidered in Assisi work should be finished with a hemstitched hem or with four-sided stitch. If four-sided stitch is used the hem should be very narrow and rolled so that the finished effect is cordlike.

Fig. 7.4 Cushion embroidered in scarlet and black stranded cotton, and finished around the edge with a black and scarlet twisted cord (m *V. Payne, ETC*).

8 Appliqué

The word 'appliqué' comes from the French and means applied work. This exactly explains what is done; one piece of fabric is applied over another, and various means are used to hold the edges down.

In ancient times rich hangings were embroidered in this way by the Greeks and Egyptians. The Egyptian figure friezes are typical examples. In the Middle Ages the Crusaders had coats, tents and horse-cloths embroidered with appliqué designs similar to the arms on the curtains shown in Fig. 8.1. Throughout the centuries this work has been used for church banners and vestments, as well as for heraldic and ecclesiastical embroideries which have often used fabulous fabrics and delicate stitchery. In more recent years the Indians and

Fig. 8.1 Lanercost Priory door curtains (*Rev. R. Lindsay, M.A.; Cumberland News*).

Persians have done a great deal of this work, often using it to imitate richer and more intricate embroideries.

Appliqué work is ideal if you want to obtain a quick, bold effect. It is an excellent type of embroidery for covering large areas, and can be very gay for wall panels, pictures, curtains, fire screens and similar furnishings; though small mats are a useful introduction to design for this type of work. The curtains shown in Fig. 8.1 were embroidered for Lanercost Priory, Cumberland. The actual curtains are of a heavy mothproof overcoat material, grey with an almost imperceptible orange fleck to match the texture of the stonework. The story of the Priory is told in heraldic fashion by the eighteen coats of arms. Appliqué is most suitable for heavy curtains of this type, and is not suitable for articles that will have to be frequently laundered.

The design is of the utmost importance. However simple it is, it must be well planned, with good colours. Bold, simple shapes are the most effective, and the smaller details should be added by stitchery after the appliqué has been worked. Geometrical designs can be made by folding and cutting paper. Take a square or circular piece of paper and fold it diagonally three times, then cut out small pieces and unfold. This method can be used for very simple appliqué patterns (Fig. 8.2).

There are several types of appliqué, and almost any fabric can be used, different methods being employed for the various fabrics. If the article is not to be washed, several kinds of material can be used on the same piece of work. For example, for a wall hanging, velvet, silk, taffeta, net and cotton could be used on a woollen background. Almost any material can be used for the ground, but it should be of an interesting colour and texture. Firm materials with clean-cut edges that do not fray too much are easiest to apply. Velvet, taffeta, firm cotton, shantung and linen are easily handled, but felt, American cloth and oiled silk have the added advantage that they do not fray at all, so that the edges need not be completely covered. For cushions, the pieces must be firmly fixed around all the edges, but pictures, hangings or fire screens need only a few embroidery stitches to attach the pieces lightly. In all appliqué work it is essential that every piece of applied fabric should be cut with the warp and weft corresponding to the warp and weft of the background. If this is not done the applied pieces may stretch or pull and become out of shape.

Material that is inclined to fray easily, or stretch out of shape, can be thinly pasted on the back and allowed to dry thoroughly. A mixture of a little gum arabic or resin and cold water should be made, then brought slowly to the boil, stirring all the time. It should be allowed to cool before use. For fragile or transparent fabrics take a piece of tissue-paper or muslin and paste it sparingly with a very thin solution of cold paste made from wheat flour. Be sure that there are no lumps and use only a very thin smear, just enough to stick the tissue-paper or muslin to the wrong side of the fabric that is to be applied. Be careful that the paste does not penetrate to the right side of the fabric so that spots are visible. Lay the fabric quite flat on the tissue-paper or muslin, and press flat with a clean cloth. Cover with several layers of clean paper, and put between two drawing boards to press for a day or two until quite dry. When appliquéing thin fabrics it is best to tack them in place and sew around them before cutting away the extra fabric.

Any threads can be used for outlining the work; the thickness should vary with the texture of the material being used. Cottons and silks of all kinds are suitable, and

Fig. 8.2 Pattern made by paper cutting. Suitable for the lid of a box, it could be worked in inlay, or felt appliqué.

Fig. 8.3

wools can be very effective for bold work. Most appliqué work can be done in the hand, but for very large pieces a frame may help.

Blind Appliqué is the name given to appliqué which has very little added embroidery. The pieces applied are secured by small back stitches, or blind stitches. Plain materials are usually used. It is a very simple, quick way of decorating articles, and is especially suitable for big pieces of work such as bedspreads and curtains. Each piece of material is cut out with narrow turnings, and pinned and tacked in place. The raw edges of the fabric can be tucked under with the point of the needle, and slipstitched in position with ordinary, matching thread. Fig. 8.3 shows a simple design for blind appliqué, which could decorate a child's playsuit. Black and white appliqué were used on lime sailcloth.

Figure appliqué is very similar to blind appliqué, but satin stitch is used around the edges instead of slipstitch. Minute satin stitches are worked so close together that the stitches touch each other. The raw edges can either be tucked in with the needle, or satin stitch can be worked around the outline before the fabric is cut away very close to the stitching. Any extra embroidery is worked after the applied pieces have been fixed.

Hemmed appliqué It is possible to fix firm materials down with ordinary hemming stitches, using a fine thread in self-colour. The edges should first be turned under to prevent fraying.

Hemstitched appliqué Simple geometrical designs cut on the thread of the material can be applied with hemstitching, the edges being turned under first. This can sometimes be very effective, especially on table linen (Fig. 8.4).

Appliqué for lingerie Net is often appliquéd to lingerie,

replacing silk or nylon as part of the garment. Lightly
draw or transfer the design on to the right or wrong side
of the silk. Tack a piece of net on the wrong side of the
material but extending beyond the design. Outline the
design with small running stitches, then work over these
stitches with very close overcasting, or buttonholing. The
loops of the buttonhole stitches should come on the inside
as this is the edge that will be cut away. When the design
is outlined, cut away the fabric of the garment leaving the
net in its place. On the reverse side of the garment cut
away the surplus net which is outside the stitching.

A net hem is effective in lingerie. The net should be
placed lengthways along the hem so that it will not
stretch when it is worked. Coffee or écru net looks well as
an edging on white, pink or blue fabric.

Another type of appliqué is best used on satin. The
pattern, which is also of satin, is then applied using the
wrong or dull side of the material on the shiny side of
the garment, or vice versa. This type of appliqué is usually
outlined with matching silk. Fig. 8.5 gives suitable
designs.

Appliqué on net or tulle A very dainty effect can sometimes be achieved by applying one piece of net or tulle
on top of another. A bold, clear design is needed, and this
should be firmly drawn on a piece of calico. Indian ink
can be used for the outline to make it very distinct. The
two layers of net are then tacked to the calico. Outline
the design with chain stitch, going through both pieces of
net, then trim away the under layer of net outside the
stitching. Remove from the calico and press.

Carrickmacross appliqué is a very old type of Irish
embroidery, resembling net appliqué. It has been worked
for over two hundred years and was at one time called
Carrickmacross Lace. At first very fine cambric or 'Mull'

Fig. 8.5 Patterns for appliqué on
satin lingerie.

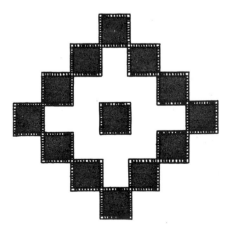

Fig. 8.4

Fig. 8.6 *The Birdcage* appliqué panel (dm *C. M. Howard; CoID*).

muslin was used with fine machine net. The design is drawn on calico as for net appliqué, then a layer of net and a layer of organdie are tacked on top of the calico, the design showing through the two layers. Using a very fine cotton (No. 100) closely overcast a thick thread of the same colour (No. 30), stitching through both the organdie and the net. When the work is finished use a pair of sharp embroidery scissors and carefully trim away the organdie outside the pattern, leaving a background of net (Fig. 8.7).

During the Irish famine of 1846 a Lace School was started on the Shirley and Bath Estates to give employment. Carrickmacross guipure was started here, no net being used, the 'fond' or background being filled with buttonholed and picotted bars. Sometimes the two methods, appliqué and guipure were most effectively used together. Designs tended to be naturalistic and floral. Often the shamrock was used, and in Victorian times the English rose and Scottish thistle were popular.

Appliqué pictures or hangings are fun to do, and any fabric can be used. Collect as wide a range of scraps as possible, and then choose pieces whose pattern or texture suggests the object you wish to represent. Cut out all the shapes in paper first, carefully marking the way the grain should go. This is most important as all the pieces applied should run the same way as the background material. Next use these pieces of paper as patterns to cut out fabric. Place the fabric pieces in position on the background, juggle them around until you have an arrangement which satisfies you, then pin them in place. Tack them along the edges, which can either be neatened by using the zig-zag attachment on the sewing-machine, or fastened down with embroidery stitches, such as blanket stitch, herringbone or Roumanian stitch. For a picture

Fig. 8.7 Mat of Carrickmacross appliqué, in coffee organdie and net (m *J. Foreman, ETC*).

that is later to be covered with glass the raw edges need not be turned in. Lines of embroidery can then be worked to link the main shapes, or around the outlines as an echo.

Fig. 8.6 shows an appliqué panel in which a variety of fabrics and stitches have been used, Fig. 8.9 another panel made from a wide variety of fabrics and stitches and including braids, metallic threads and sequins.

Shadow appliqué on organdie can be most effective and very dainty. The design should be traced on to the appliqué material, which is usually organdie, and cut out, allowing for a small turning all round the outline. These pieces are then tacked on the back of the work, matching the warp and weft threads of the applied pieces with those of the background. Tack around each piece. Outline the design with very small running stitches, and then whip over these, or work chain stitch or pinstitch along the line. The extra organdie is then cut away close to the stitching, and any surface embroidery added. Interesting effects can be obtained by applying several layers of organdie or net. Fig. 8.8 shows an Embroiderers' Guild Transfer, which would look well carried out in this way.

Inlay work This is a reversal of appliqué work. It was widely used in ecclesiastical hangings and vestments centuries ago. There are some very beautiful examples in the Victoria and Albert Museum. The background fabric is cut away in a pattern to show a different colour lining underneath; in some cases the background as well as the pattern is cut out and laid on another background. Simple conventional designs are the best, as only two colours are used; there should be no details. Counter-change designs lend themselves to this treatment. The fabrics used should be those that do not fray easily. In

Fig. 8.9. *Madonna with a Flower* appliqué panel (dm *Dorothy A. Allsop; CoID*).

Fig. 8.8 Design for shadow appliqué (*EG*).

Fig. 8.10

church work velvets are frequently used, while felt and leather are also excellent for the purpose. Fig. 8.10 gives a design that could well be carried out in felt inlay work. When widely different textures are used, the thinner ones should be backed with another fabric to make them more equal in weight.

Decoupé work is the name sometimes given to modern inlay work; it is very popular on the Continent. Linens of contrasting colours are used, the uppermost layer being cut away in places to reveal the under layer. Sometimes different coloured pieces of linen are used as the under layer in different parts of the design.

9 Ayrshire work

Towards the end of the eighteenth century, Luigi Ruffini, an Italian merchant, came to Edinburgh, and visited many of the haberdashers of the city, showing them samples of the beautiful Dresden work (Fig. 9.1). He was a skilled embroiderer himself, and his plan was to start a workroom in Scotland and train his own apprentices to do this type of embroidery. He pointed out that as no threads were withdrawn from the fabric, it was in no way weakened by the embroidery. Foreign lace was much in demand at that time as it was used lavishly in the costume of the wealthy, and many attempts had been made to foster lace-making in Scotland, but one of the difficulties had been getting thread which was as fine as that used on the Continent. Many of the influential businessmen of Edinburgh thought Ruffini's proposition was a possible way of satisfying the ever-increasing demand for this type of lace, and he was granted a small sum of money to start his work. He began with about twenty young apprentices mostly between eight and ten years of age. He taught them the skill of this fine embroidery, in exchange for their keep. There was immediately a big demand for their work, and Ruffini took on more and more apprentices.

Unfortunately, very fine linen such as was needed for the Dresden pulled work was difficult to obtain in Edinburgh. Earlier in the century weavers had come over from the Low Countries, and started weaving this fine cambric in Scotland, but it was still in short supply, and more expensive than the continental fabrics. The trade of the East India Company was, however, just beginning to have an effect on the Western world, and fine cotton goods were being brought home from the Far East. These were soon copied in Europe.

Inspired by the muslins which had come from Dacca the first good quality muslin was hand-woven in Paisley towards the end of the eighteenth century, and was used for dainty aprons. Fine fabrics were very fashionable at this time, and the new muslin sold rapidly at a good price, often as much as 9s or 9s 6d a yard. Soon the west of Scotland was known for its delicate muslins. A white muslin dress became the height of fashion, and the new water supplies which were being installed in wealthy houses solved the problem of laundering these gowns. Ruffini's apprentices had at last a plentiful supply of material for their embroidery. By the end of the eighteenth century the war with France had entirely stopped the imports of foreign muslins and laces, and the demand for Scottish work increased.

Fig. 9.1 Dresden work—the corner of a kerchief (lent by *R. H. A. Swain*).

Some of the fabrics imported from the East were richly embroidered, and several of the embroiderers in England and Scotland began to copy these exquisite floral designs. The Schools of Art in Scotland encouraged young designers to design for the new industry and prizes were offered for the best work submitted. The fine muslin was stretched over a hoop or frame and the girls would 'dot' or 'flower' it with tiny sprays. Fine-pulled work could be worked as fillings for the sprigs, while chain stitch was used for outlining.

The fashionable dresses of the time often had a wide panel of embroidery running up from the bottom hem, and babies' christening robes were lavishly worked, the designs becoming ever more elaborate as time passed.

In 1814 a young widow returned to her home in Ayrshire with a lovely French christening robe embroidered with needlepoint lace stitches. She employed a small group of women and taught them how to embroider muslin using these stitches; from this began a new type of Ayrshire work of very high quality, even more skilled than the tambour work done by Ruffini's apprentices. A beading stitch was used for outlining the design, and unlike the earlier work, no drawn fabric stitches were used. Lace stitch fillings were worked on drawn threadwork backgrounds. The christening robes—a popular product—had a triangular panel down the front, richly embroidered and similar in style to the adult dresses of the period. Fig. 9.2 gives the detail of one of these panels.

Later, much of this work was done in Ireland and sold as Ayrshire work. Later still, towards the middle of the nineteenth century, the vine crop failed in Madeira, and a Scotswoman there taught some of the peasants to do this work to help them find money. As it was so hot in Madeira, the work would often become damp with the

Fig. 9.2 Detail of the front panel of
a christening robe in Ayrshire
embroidered muslin (*RSM*).

Fig. 10.1 The Elizabethan Falkland cover. Linen is embroidered with black silk in back, chain, button-hole, braid and coral stitches (*V & A —crown copyright*).

Fig. 10.2 Samples of blackwork designs.

workers' moist hands, and the design, which was in blue, would soil the muslin. It therefore became common for the people out there to work with a blue thread, and the production of the blue Madeira work became a small industry.

Twenty years later the fashion had again changed and muslin was no longer the vogue. The new bustle needed firmer, stiffer fabrics, new dyes had been invented, and heavier, darker fabrics took the place of the dainty muslins. Some twenty years before this, the Swiss had invented a machine that made embroidery, and with this they began copying the Ayrshire white work. By 1870 a steady decline in Ayrshire embroidery had already set in, and by the end of the century it was complete. During the sixty to seventy years when this embroidery had flourished, some wonderful work had been produced, and many of the christening robes are still preserved and cherished in British museums and by families who have handed them down from generation to generation.

10 Blackwork

Blackwork first became popular in England in Queen Elizabeth I's reign. Catherine of Aragon is said to have introduced it at the beginning of the sixteenth century. This technique of working with black threads on fine white linen was much in use in Spain at that time, and is sometimes known even today as Spanish work. Portraits

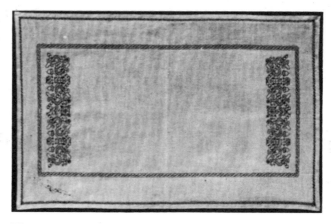

Fig. 10.3 Cream linen table-runner (m *M. Graham, ETC*).

of Henry VIII which are to be seen in the National Portrait Gallery and in Hampton Court give us an example of the beautiful contemporary blackwork. Many of these portraits were painted by Holbein and this type of stitchery is often known as 'Holbein work'. It was largely used as a decoration on dresses and was also seen on undergarments of both men and women.

The Falkland Cover and Pillow (Fig. 10.1) are among the best examples of this work and may be seen in the Victoria and Albert Museum. In this design the bunches of grapes are beautifully handled, to give varying qualities and many tones. The outlines are well defined, and make an interesting contrast to their half-toned fillings. The proportion of the dark solids to the other tones is well balanced. Many of the sixteenth-century designs were taken from the woodcuts and engravings which illustrate the contemporary herbals and the printed pattern books. One can imagine the interest and excitement felt by those lucky enough to own, or even see, one of the newly printed books, and no doubt the ladies of the time eagerly seized upon this fresh inspiration for embroidery. In this country a particularly English style of design developed, using flowers, birds, beasts and insect motifs. The fillings sometimes included fine seeding and speckling, and sometimes a gold thread was used with the black.

This type of stitchery is also found on work from Egypt and most of the Mediterranean countries.

Some beautiful border and corner designs in blackwork can be taken from samplers in museums. These look most effective worked on tray-cloths, runners or table-cloths (Figs. 10.2 to 10.6).

In making or choosing a design for blackwork see that the size of the shapes is varied. Large, open shapes show the pattern textures to advantage; well placed shapes

Fig. 10.5 Cream linen cushion (m J. Lawrence, ETC).

Fig. 10.6 Detail of Fig. 10.4.

Fig. 10.4

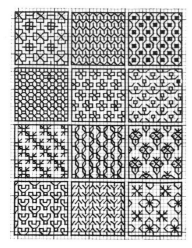

Fig. 10.7

Fig. 10.8 Blackwork fillings used to form a picture.

allow the darks to contrast with the light-toned ground and the varied half-tones. An outline design of various leaf shapes is a good beginning, each shape having a different filling.

The quiet restraint of the late sixteenth-century blackwork appeals to many people today, and there is a real thrill to be found in inventing new fillings, worked on the counted threads of evenly woven linen. Fig. 10.7 shows some of these fillings worked out on graph paper. The black silk used on traditional work was hand-spun and hand-dyed, often slightly unevenly, and was usually a brownish black. Threads today are so intensely black that an interesting effect can be obtained by using several shades—nigger brown, very dark blue, very dark green and black. A Filoselle silk or stranded cotton is the best to use as the number of threads can then be varied to give different tones.

The formal patterns are made up of running stitches, worked entirely by the thread on the linen, working one way, then coming back over the pattern, filling in the alternate stitches to make a double running or back stitch effect. If this is done the pattern is alike on both sides.

11 Broderie Anglaise

Broderie Anglaise is a dainty type of work, sometimes known as English white embroidery. It really originated in Czechoslovakia where it is worked in brilliant colours as well as in white, and is used to decorate aprons and the sleeves of the dresses worn as the national costume. It was first known in this country in the late eighteenth and early nineteenth centuries, when it was used on underclothes, dresses, caps, babies' clothes and household linen. Many babies' caps and christening robes are still preserved in British museums. Usually this work was done on white cotton or linen, with a matching thread, but occasionally a contrasting colour was used on household linen, and sometimes a blue, white or brown thread was used on a natural fabric. In this early work no surface embroidery was used. The stems of flowers were worked in various sized eyelets, and a tremendous amount of labour went into the work.

Very few types of stitches are used, pierced or cut-out shapes being overcast around the edges to form flower or leaf shapes. The designs are small and simple, consisting of tiny flowers made from eyelets, which can be round or oval, and leaves worked in the same way. Later, satin stitch was used, and stems and lines were worked in stem stitch, chain stitch or overcasting.

Variations of Broderie Anglaise are Swiss embroidery, or Madeira work. In this work, more surface embroidery is introduced, the eyelets and cut flower shapes being linked by stems and other details in satin stitch, stem stitch or overcasting. The introduction of this surface work made it much quicker to get an attractive effect.

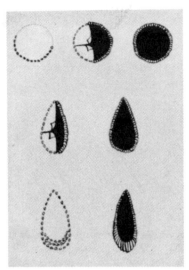

Fig. 11.1

Fig. 11.2 The design shown below worked on cotton lawn (m *A. Loveridge, ETC*).

Fig. 11.3 Design for white work similar to those used in the eighteenth century.

Madeira work which is done on the Island, often has most elaborate details, and is worked on a cream or écru background with a deeper shade of thread.

Broderie Anglaise is a suitable decoration for underclothes, blouses or children's clothes.

In designing remember to leave space for the outlining of each shape, for example, the petals of a flower must not be placed too close together or when the outlining has been worked they will touch one another. Leaves are often similar in shape to the petals of flowers, and are cut in the same way. Designs made for lazy daisy stitch can often be adapted for this work.

If you are going to do Broderie Anglaise you will need a pair of sharp scissors, fine embroidery needles, and a stiletto for making the eyelets. Firm, smooth fabrics that will not fray too much should be used. Fine linen, cotton lawn, cambric or nainsock is suitable for most articles, though pure silk, or crêpe-de-chine may be preferred for underclothes. This work used to be done only in white, but recent practice favours any pale colour. Stranded cottons or pure silk thread should be used.

It is best to work a fine running stitch around each circle (two rows for large eyelets) before beginning to embroider. To make a small hole, use a stiletto to pierce the material; for a larger one cut across the hole diagonally in both directions, then turn the small pieces of fabric to the wrong side. Next make very tiny overcasting stitches over the running line, drawing the fabric back to form an even hole. When you have finished the stitching, any edges of fabric remaining on the wrong side can be cut away. Fig. 11.1 illustrates how these holes are worked. When it is wished to vary in shape the overcasting at one end, several rows of running stitch should first be worked at that end. Larger areas of cut work are sometimes introduced, and bars are worked to bridge the gaps.

Spots or dots in the surface embroidery should be padded by first working a circle of satin stitch on each, then working on top of this satin stitch the opposite way.

The edges of Broderie Anglaise are often scalloped; a padded effect is achieved by using chain instead of running stitch underneath the buttonholing.

12 Canvas work

Fig. 11.4 Some designs for Broderie Anglaise.

Canvas work consists of stitches worked upon canvas, completely covering the whole surface with embroidery to give the effect of a tapestry. This work is, therefore, sometimes called tapestry work or petit point. It is very soothing to do as, once the work is planned, it consists merely of the repetition of a few stitches worked over the canvas. A very hard-wearing form of embroidery, it has for centuries been widely used in furnishings, with few variations except in design.

Canvas stitches form part of the design of the famous Syon Cope, now to be seen in the Victoria and Albert Museum. In Tudor times small motifs were used, often small flowers on cushions and coverings. Coats-of-arms and heraldic designs were also common. During Elizabeth I's reign wall hangings, bedcovers, cushions and valances were worked in petit point. The designs often consisted of a central panel containing a figure. This panel would be

surrounded by strapwork or the garter. The garter itself
was often sub-divided into panels each with decorative
fillings of birds, beasts and trees. Towards the end of this
period Hungarian point work also became popular.

In Jacobean times the patterns used were large and
ornate, consisting of stylised plants and animals which
were worked in wool on heavy twill hangings. Under the
Stuarts pictures became fashionable. The embroiderer
would often use Biblical themes, and dress the characters
in costumes of the period. Simple drawings of the king
and queen were also common. The reign of William and
Mary saw a change to large flowing designs which were
used to embroider the backs and seats of chairs. By the
beginning of the eighteenth century a strong oriental
influence was much in evidence. Naturalistic designs
were used on dark backgrounds—often huge baskets or
vases of flowers were worked with delicate shading. These
tapestry embroideries were frequently used to upholster
the large, winged arm-chairs which then were in vogue.
The Georgian era saw yet another change, the embroidery
becoming heavier to suit the popular heavy mahogany
furniture. Pictorial panels and floral designs were enclosed in scroll work, foliage or flowers, all of which show
the strong contemporary Chinese influence.

The great furniture makers of the late eighteenth and
early nineteenth centuries were famous for their beautiful
chairs which were enhanced by the tapestry work used
in the upholstery. The designs on Chippendale chairs were
often in the Gothic style; they consisted of a central
panel, containing a stylised tree, with flowers and birds.
Hepplewhite furniture was much lighter in style than
Chippendale, and the needlework designs were daintier;
often bands or stripes of daintily embroidered flowers
formed ribbons across the background. By the late

eighteenth century, Sheraton was at work, making most of his furniture from satinwood. Again the Gothic influence can be seen in the tapestry work designs which often consist of dainty arches and pillars enclosing beautifully shaded flowers. In the latter half of the nineteenth century Berlin work was popular, and the Victorians worked a vast number of pictures and floral designs to use in their homes.

Tapestry work has been used not only for chair seats, stool tops, fire screens and carpets, but often, too, for huge wall hangings. The Hatton Garden Hangings (Fig. 12.1), in the Victoria and Albert Museum, are beautiful examples of this. They were discovered behind the wallpaper in an old house in Hatton Garden where they had probably been since the middle of the seventeenth century. The designs are typical of that period, incorporating huge leaves and flowers, and consisting of six large panels with foliage at the top and containing many easily recognisable birds and animals. The different stitches include Goblein rococo, Hungarian, rice and tent.

There are many interesting tapestries all over the country. One can be seen in Notgrove Parish Church in the Cotswolds. Consisting of seventeen strips formed into one canvas, it is a harmonious piece of work which was designed by Sir Colin Anderson in 1936 and was finished in 1954, having been left untouched during the war years. Two generations of the family worked upon it, both men and women. Parts of the border were worked by the villagers, and Sir Colin himself worked the landscapes. This hanging, unlike the Hatton Garden Hangings, is worked in gros point and petit point.

In recent years canvas work has been used in many churches. One of the churches that has inspired many workers to take up this type of embroidery is the

Fig. 12.1 Wall hanging from Hatton Garden dating from the middle of the seventeenth century. Canvas is worked with wools in petit point, Hungarian point, cross, rice and star stitches, and with eyelet holes (*V & A—crown copyright*).

seven-hundred-year-old Church of All Saints, Chelsea.
Over two hundred kneelers have been embroidered for this
church in recent years, especially during the reconstruc-
tion which followed its demolition by a bomb in 1941. The
church is rich in history, and each kneeler has been
designed and worked in memory of some past parishioner.
In order to achieve some uniformity, each one consists
of a central panel, with a Maltese cross in each corner,
but otherwise there is a wide variety of designs. Following this example, Guildford Cathedral and many parish
churches throughout the country are using embroidery of
this type to beautify their buildings. One of the kneelers
which has been worked for the clergy of St John's
Church, Eastbourne, is shown in Fig. 12.2.

Kneelers for a church should measure 13 to 15 in. long
and 10 in. wide. Pads can be stuffed with horsehair, or be
mounted as the Chelsea ones are, on Dunlopillo cushions,
two thicknesses being used, with the smooth surfaces at
the top and bottom. Such cushions should always be
enclosed in a cotton covering before the embroidery is
mounted. Good linen canvas should be used; eleven holes
to the inch is ideal.

Canvas work is used today not only for tapestries, church
kneelers and alms bags, but in the home for chair seats,
stool tops, pictures, and carpets, while very attractive
evening bags can be made in silk. Sometimes the design
is painted on the canvas, but the best method of working
is to follow, by counting the threads, a design which has
been worked out on graph paper, each square representing a stitch. Colour can add greatly to the charm of this
work. Several shades of the same colour used for a background give additional richness, though care needs to be
taken to keep the same direction of stitch throughout the
work. Sometimes a background is worked in two very

similar shades or it is possible to have two threads in the same needle and work with this double thread.

Embroidery on canvas is intended to strengthen as well as decorate. Wool, cotton or silk can be used, each giving an entirely different effect. Loosely woven, coarse linen was used in the past, but later on special canvas was woven for the purpose. Today there is a wide range of canvases, the coarsest having only five threads to the inch, and the finest as many as forty threads. The best quality canvas has 'polished threads', each thread being separated and rounded. In recent years double thread canvas has been used; this makes it easier to see which part to take up in stitching. The single-thread canvas is used for petit point and Hungarian work, but the other stitches can be worked on the double canvas.

A blunt tapestry needle should be used. For fine work stranded cottons or Filoselle is sometimes suitable, though wool is more usual. A very wide range of colours is available in tapestry wool, and different ply can be used to suit the canvas. It is important to buy all the wool for the background before beginning the work, as sometimes colours vary slightly and it may prove difficult to match a thread. Two or even three strands of thread may be required, as it is very important to achieve the correct thickness. If the thread is too thin the mesh will show through; if it is too thick it will make the work look bulky and puckered. It is always best to experiment first with a small piece of the canvas. Use the thread the right way, that is, the surface should feel smooth as you draw your finger along from the needle to the fabric. Use only a short length of thread, as working with a single pull makes the tension more even and the thread does not become roughened, frayed, or thinner in use.

Prepare the canvas before beginning work by cutting

Fig. 12.2 Church kneeler (d *E. Morfe*, m *I. Strudwick*).

Fig. 12.3 Evening bag embroidered in stranded cottons (m *Author*).

an overlap of about 2 in. all round, and carefully over-sewing the edges. For large pieces of work a frame should be used. The needle should be pushed through the canvas with the right hand and sent straight up again by the left hand, which is held underneath, a thimble being used on each hand.

When starting, or joining in a new thread, tie a knot in the thread, take it down leaving a long stitch at the back, and bring it out in a place that will be covered by stitches. Work over this long stitch and when the knot is reached cut it off. In this way the back of the work is kept neat and loose ends are prevented. To finish, darn the end into the back of some of the stitches. If several different colours are being used each thread can be temporarily left without unthreading the needle or finishing off, then darned into the back to reappear where it is needed again.

Tent stitch is one of the simplest stitches and is made by working over each thread where the warp and weft threads cross. This stitch often used to be called petit point; being small and flexible it can be used for tiny detail such as the shading of faces or figures. The evening bag shown in Fig. 12.3 was worked in this stitch, so that the flowers could be shaded.

Cross stitch gives a rough surface. It is sometimes worked one way in tent stitch, the crosses being com-pleted on the return journey. Cross stitch with variations, and rice stitch, are very strong, and are therefore useful in making church kneelers. Florentine, long-armed cross and eye stitches are good for large areas as they give an interesting variety of textures.

Goblein stitch gives a smooth texture and is good as a background stitch or for shaded areas. Hungarian or cushion stitch is a form of satin stitch used for background fillings. Montenegrin cross stitch is different on each side and is a pretty stitch to use when both sides of the work are to be seen.

When finished, canvas work should be stretched. This is most important as the canvas pulls out of shape in working. The back of the canvas should be damped, then pulled carefully into shape, and pinned face down on a pad of blotting paper. If, after being left to dry for a few days, it has not been restored to its correct shape, it should again be stretched. A good strong paste can be rubbed into the wrong side of kneelers, or carpets, to help keep the work in shape and make it wear longer.

13 Cross stitch

Cross stitch is one of the oldest and most popular forms of embroidery. It originated in the Coptic period, was well known in ancient China, and in later years spread through India to Greece, Egypt, and ancient Rome. In medieval times nuns all over Europe practised this type of embroidery. Wonderful work was done in Burgundy in the fourteenth century, but soon after, the skill began to decline. The peasants, however, continued the craft, passing it on through the generations, until, in the early nineteenth century, the quality of their work was recognised and it became admired throughout the world. Much of their embroidery was extremely fine, some even being worked with human hair on the finest

Fig. 13.1 Cross stitch design from Jugoslavia, worked in scarlet, black, green and gold.

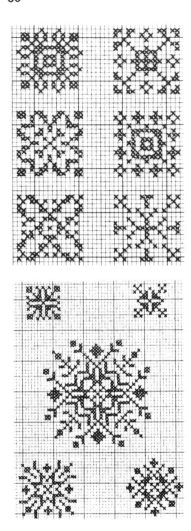

Figs. 13.2a and b

linen. Over the centuries certain colour schemes became traditional, though these varied from one country or even one district to another. A bright deep red was often used with deep blue, other patterns were frequently worked in red and black, blue and black, or black, brown and yellow. Animals, and plants were represented symbolically. Different areas specialised in certain designs, but often a design was taken to another country by pilgrims or invading soldiers returning home. Peasant women frequently kept a strip of linen and embroidered on it any little motif which attracted them. Sometimes the richly embroidered dress of a court lady would inspire a peasant who would copy a motif from it onto her sampler, to use later in embroidering an apron or blouse. As the courts of Europe moved from place to place the same designs would find their way into the peasant embroideries of many different countries.

Early designs from the Holy Land are rectangular, and use geometric symbols, whereas farther east the forms are more naturalistic, being built round stylised flowers, birds, or beasts. The Greek Holy Cross and the Star of Bethlehem inspired innumerable patterns. In recent years great efforts have been made in Czechoslovakia and other Central European countries to preserve the folk art, and some beautiful pieces of peasant embroidery are being worked and treasured. Peasant costumes in these Slav countries are richly embroidered on the sleeves, belts, pockets, around the hem of the skirts and on blouses and boleros. Most of these patterns are in cross stitch, worked on very thin muslin in vivid colours, red blue, gold and black being the most popular. Household linen in these countries is also gaily decorated with fine stitchery. In Sicily very fine cross stitch is worked over two threads of fine linen. Lively figures of people and

Fig. 13.3 Stool top embroidered in a traditional peasant design with black cross stitch (m *Author*).

animals as well as flowers are worked in gay colours. In Montenegro you will find a variation of cross stitch known as Montenegrin cross stitch.

In this country cross stitch was for many centuries widely used on ecclesiastical vestments and in heraldry. Parts of the famous Syon Cope (Victoria and Albert Museum) are worked in cross stitch. This stitch was also used on Victorian samplers, many of which were worked by young children. Fine cotton and thread were used to make cross-stitch pictures, or to mark out a verse, then the sampler was signed and dated by the embroiderer.

Today cross stitch is one of the most popular types of embroidery, partly because it is so easy to do, and partly because it can be used on almost any article. One stitch only is used and the beauty of the work depends largely on colour, and on the regularity of the stitch. Tray-cloths, trolley-cloths, guest towels, cushions, table-cloths, tea-cosies, table-mats, runners, or bedspreads can be embroidered with it, while it is suitable for decorating blouses, aprons, children's dresses or sunsuits.

Design and colour are of the utmost importance in this type of work. It is better to choose a good design and adapt it, than to use one which will give a disappointing result. It is also vital to remember in planning the background that the shapes left between the masses in the pattern are as important as the pattern itself. Consider too the effect of massed colour, and not of individual stitches. Beautiful designs can be seen in the Victoria and Albert Museum. Other sources of inspiration are good books on peasant embroidery, and the vast number of beautiful traditional designs which the embroiderer can adapt for her own purpose. Designs can easily be worked out on graph paper (Figs. 13.2a and b) and the embroidery is then worked from this chart.

Fig. 13.5 Table-cloth of Danish net embroidered in cross stitch with sprigs of wild flowers (dm *Author*).

Fig. 13.4 Cushion in grey even weave linen embroidered in black, white and scarlet cross stitch (dm *D. Holdaway, ETC*).

Fig. 13.6 Alphabet in cross stitch,
useful for marking linens.

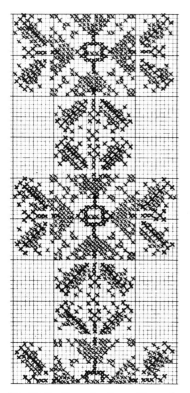

Fig. 13.7a Some border patterns for
cross stitch.

Cross stitch is most often worked by counting the threads on even-weave material. For articles such as table-cloths and cushions Glenshee or Dryad's Willow cross stitch material is ideal as the threads are even and easily counted. Danish net is best suited to fine work (Fig. 13.5). If cross stitch is to be worked on a material of which the threads cannot easily be counted, a piece of mesh canvas can be tacked over the fabric and the pattern then embroidered over the canvas and through the basic material. The stitches will need to be pulled rather tightly so that when the work is finished, the threads of the canvas can be cut and drawn out, leaving the stitchery on the background. The canvas should be cut away very near the embroidery so that only a very short thread has to be pulled through the stitches. If the canvas is stiff, it is advisable to soak it for a few hours in warm water, then dry it, before tacking it to the fabric. This makes it more pliable, but care must be taken not to pull it out of square.

Any threads can be used—wool, silk, linen or stranded cotton—but the thickness of the thread should match that of the warp thread in the background material, that is, a coarse thread must be used on a coarse material. On medium weave material two threads of stranded cotton can be used for each cross or square of graph paper. For bolder work, three threads may be used; for very fine work one will be sufficient.

When working a cross stitch border, it is best to begin in the middle and work outwards. A corner can then be obtained by placing a small mirror at an angle of 45° to the edge. The reflection in the mirror can easily be copied on graph paper before the next side is worked. Mirrors also help in forming a square motif from a straight strip of pattern. The strip is placed along one edge of the square, two mirrors are set up, one from each corner,

Fig. 13.8 Cream linen tea-cosy
embroidered with small cross stitch
motifs, using scarlet stranded cotton
(dm *M. Woolnough, ETC*).

meeting in the centre, and the square is seen. Different parts of the strip should be tried to obtain the best corner effect.

It is essential that the top stitch of cross stitch should always go the same way, left to right being most usual. When the light shines on the work it will then appear even. Crosses should be of the same size, angle and tension. If cross stitch is to be worked on an article both sides of which will be seen, for example, table napkins or guest towels, it is best to use two-sided cross stitch.

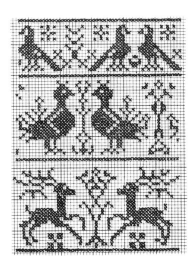

Fig. 13.7b

14 Darning

Darning is sometimes used as a simple type of embroidery. It is very easy to do as it consists of only one stitch—a running stitch of various lengths worked so that a little of the ground is picked up. Pattern darning was often used in Coptic embroideries. In the sixteenth and seventeenth centuries darning on net, or lacis work, as it was called, was popular in France and Spain. A square mesh was used for this work, and by using different darning patterns as fillings, pictures were formed. In the eighteenth and nineteenth centuries it was fashionable to make samplers in darning stitch. Some of the old samplers of the nineteenth century which are now in our museums, are worked with delicate darning patterns, and is is believed that they may have been made in order to practise the actual darning which would

Fig. 14.1 Border patterns darned on natural Glenshee linen with black-and-white Anchor Soft cotton (dm *Author*).

be used to mend damask table linen. Darning patterns were also worked on huckaback linen, and used to decorate men's waistcoats. This was a quick and easy form of embroidery as the threads were just darned in and out of the raised bars of the huckaback. Today it is widely used in Slav countries, and some beautiful designs come from Jugoslavia.

Darning on net is attractive for curtains, and white darning on nylon net can be used to make pretty wedding veils.

All types of darning may be either bold or fine. The first is carried out in coarse threads over a fairly large area. Both the ground and the pattern are worked with darning fillings which sometimes go in various directions. Here, the colour and tone of the thread are most important to the design. Fine darning is usually worked with a stranded silk, Filoselle or mercerised thread. Ivory embroidery is included in this type. It is worked on canvas, which is entirely covered with various darning fillings all in white. Sometimes the shapes are outlined with Japanese gold thread, or a coloured Filoselle thread. A single-thread canvas is used and the number of strands of silk used for the embroidery can be varied to give different thicknesses and textures. Tea-cloths, covers for blotters, books or work bags can be made from this work.

When using darning simply as a filling, choose a fine background fabric which is sufficiently loosely woven for a single thread to be picked up. Pick up only one thread and see that each row is touching the previous one so that no ground shows, and a smooth silky effect is produced.

Irregular darning is sometimes used as a filling, and in this case the lines of stitches can be farther apart so that some of the background fabric shows through. This of course is a much quicker method of working a filling and can sometimes be quite attractive if different coloured threads are used.

Pattern darning is also used on evenly woven, coarse fabrics (linen, huckaback or canvas). This is fairly quickly worked even on large areas, darning, running or tacking stitches being used as a simple decoration. Innumerable geometrical patterns can be made by varying the lengths of the stitches, and of the material picked up. Stripes, zigzags, waved lines or repeating geometrical shapes such as squares, diamonds or triangles are all suitable (Fig. 14.1). In this type of embroidery the threads are counted, each stitch being taken over a certain number of threads then under a certain number. It is essential to count the threads accurately so that the pattern is regular.

Sometimes pattern darning is used as the background to a design, leaving the motif plain. Darning in any direction can be used for a filling of this type. The motif itself is boldly outlined with a clear line stitch—chain stitch, couching or one of the whipped stitches.

Damask darning is another, more complicated form of pattern darning. It consists of running threads which are worked in two different directions. An interesting effect can be obtained by using two different colours or shades of one colour.

Diagonal darning, where the thread is carried over and under a certain number of threads in a diagonal direction, can give interesting results. A tweed effect can be obtained by a second, parallel row of stitching. Experiment with different lengths of stitch and different colour arrangements.

Double darning is alike on both sides, and is used on work from Turkey, Persia, the Greek Islands and the Near East. A running stitch is worked in one direction

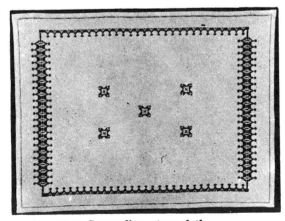

Fig. 14.2 Cream linen tray-cloth decorated with scarlet silk darning (dm *J. Pettifer, ETC*).

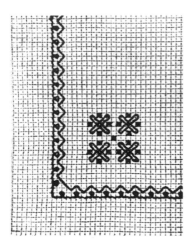

Fig. 14.3 Detail of white and blue table-cloth in lattice fabric, decorated with darning in blue Anchor Soft cotton (dm *Author*).

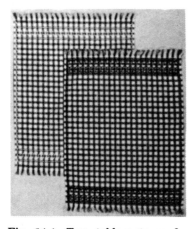

Fig. 14.4 Two table-mats made from red and white check lattice fabric, and embroidered with darning.

going over and under the same number of threads. A return journey is then made picking up the threads which were not picked up in the first journey. The needle goes in exactly the same hole on the return as was used on the first journey. The effect is one of solid horizontal bands. Sometimes it is worked with each row starting halfway along the previous one so that diagonal bands are formed.

Surface darning is sometimes used in a design. As the name implies this stitch is worked on the surface of the fabric, the stitches not being taken through in the usual way. First of all long vertical stitches are worked from top to bottom of the space to be filled. Next the horizontal stitches are made, darning over and under these threads and going through the fabric only at the beginning and end of each row. The finished result is a woven panel that is attached only at the ends. If this is worked in two colours an interesting, chequered effect is obtained. A variation of darning similar to this work comes from Jugoslavia.

Darning on lattice fabric lends itself to darning. The darning stitches are taken on the surface of the fabric going under the 'lattice' threads (Figs. 14.3 and 14.4).

15 Double running

This is one of the oldest types of embroidery—specimens have been found in the tombs of ancient Egypt. A great deal has been done in Roumania, in fact it is often called Roumanian work. A fragment of linen embroidered in blue silk double running stitch, which can now be seen in the Whitworth Art Gallery, Manchester, was made in Persia between A.D. 226 and A.D. 632. In the sixteenth century this work was widely used in Europe to decorate clothing. It is still popular in Volterra in Tuscany where it is called *Volterrano*. It has a very dainty filigree effect, and since the embroidery should look alike on both sides when it is finished, it is especially suitable for decorating table napkins, guest towels and other reversible articles. It is often combined with Assisi embroidery and in Italy it is called *St Chiara*.

The straight or zigzag designs can be drawn on graph paper (Fig. 15.1), each square representing two or three threads of the fabric, according to the thickness of the weave.

Linen with warp and weft of equal thickness is the best for this type of work. It should be sufficiently loosely woven for the threads to be easily counted.

A dark or distinctive colour is most commonly used for this work. Dark brown, navy blue, black or scarlet are often used on a white or natural ground, while deep blue or red are traditional in Roumania and Bulgaria. White, cream or natural grounds are the obvious choices, but a coral or blue ground with white embroidery is equally effective, or a coffee ground with cream stitchery.

The embroidery thread should be of about the same

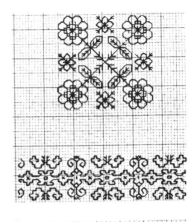

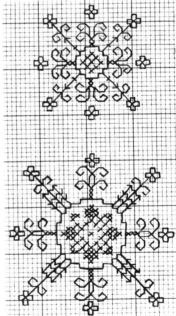

Fig. 15.1 Patterns for double running.

Fig. 15.2 Pattern taken from a Russian peasant embroidery.

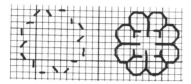

Fig. 15.3 Method of working double running motif.

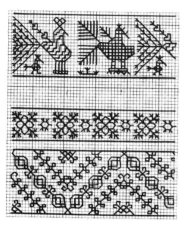

Fig. 15.4 Border designs for double running.

thickness as that of the warp. A needle with a blunt point is the easiest to use.

Double running consists of working one way, going over and under counted threads, and on the way back filling in the gaps between the stitches. It is advisable to find the main line of the pattern and follow this along on the first journey, then on the return journey work all the off shoots (Fig. 15.3). On the return journey the needle should be inserted above the previous stitch and come out below the end of it, in order to form a continuous line. To fasten on one should very carefully darn over and under a few threads which will be covered by the first stitch, and finishing off can be done on the wrong side by carefully darning back for a few threads. Ordinary back stitch will suffice on cushions or any articles that are to be lined when finished, as it can be worked straight along without regard for the appearance on the wrong side. Before beginning to work a border pattern, the corner should be worked out with the aid of a small pocket mirror placed at an angle of 45° to the border line.

Double running is often combined with cross stitch; this work is known as Holbein work as many of Holbein's portraits show costume embroidered in this way. Some of the delicate designs of this period were based on the Tudor rose. Another simple design often used was the Greek Key pattern, embellished with little side sprigs. In other reigns, filligree jewellery and wrought-iron gates have inspired beautiful patterns. Fig. 15.2 gives a pattern taken from a Russian peasant embroidery which uses these two stitches.

The tea-cosy in Fig. 15.5 was worked in white on a coral ground, using only a single strand of cotton. The design was inspired by an old Chinese sampler, and can be adapted in many ways for different purposes.

Fig. 15.5 Tea-cosy of coral linen embroidered in white double running (m B. J. Stanley, ETC).

16 Drawn threadwork

Drawn threadwork, which consists of stitches worked upon certain threads after others have been withdrawn, gives a simple delicate effect. A good quality linen is ideal but this work can also be done on silk or cotton. It is probably one of the oldest forms of embroidery. Some of the work mentioned in the Bible—fine linen for vestments and the hangings for the Temple—was no doubt embroidered in drawn threadwork. Beautiful work was later done in Spain, Italy and Sicily, Greece, Russia and Germany.

Drawn threadwork is widely used today in peasant embroideries in Scandinavia, Hungary and the Slav countries where it is often used on traditional costume. In these central European countries very bright colours are used for drawn threadwork but the Sicilian work is usually done in white or natural.

In the late sixteenth century much of this work was done by wealthy gentlewomen who used drawn threadwork, together with lace stitches, on their household linen and on some of their garments. Many of the point lace stitches and Reticella stitches became associated with this work, being used to make decorative fillings for the open spaces. Fig. 16.2 shows two borders of drawn threadwork; both are English early eighteenth century.

This work can be used for decorating handkerchiefs, lingerie, sheets, table-cloths, tray-cloths, table napkins, table-mats, towels or pillowcases.

Any type of fabric can be used, but it is easiest to work one of even-weave. Some adjustment can be made in the number of threads drawn, however, if the threads one

Fig. 16.1a Hemstitching.

Fig. 16.1b Simple bar border.

Fig. 16.1c Zigzag border.

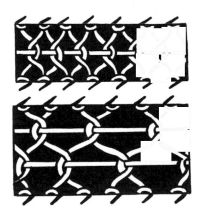

Fig. 16.1d Twisted borders.

Fig. 16.2 Borders of drawn threadwork (*V & A—crown copyright*).

way are thicker than they are the other. Drawn thread-work should always be done before any other type of embroidery, since it is essential that the work should be quite straight and flat so that the threads can be counted accurately.

There are several kinds of drawn threadwork. The simplest usually takes the form of borders; the threads of either the weft or the warp are withdrawn, and hem-stitching is used. Drawn threadwork is usually self-coloured, the embroidery thread being of the same colour or just a shade darker or lighter, and a little coarser than the warp threads of the background fabric. The thread used for hemstitching or working the bars should be smooth and finer than that used for any surface embroidery.

Hemstitching

The simplest, basic stitch, used in all kinds of drawn threadwork, is hemstitching. It has any number of varia-tions. The threads are first cut in the middle of the border, and carefully drawn back as far as the border is to go, then darned back neatly, as for needleweaving. Open-work borders are always first hemstitched so that the threads are grouped together into clusters. There are many different ways of grouping them and of linking the groups. Where two borders meet at the corners a square is formed; this should be buttonholed. A spider's web method of treating a corner is shown in Fig. 16.3. Fig. 16.1 shows simple hemstitching, and then hemstitching to group the threads into bars and zigzags. After the straight bars have been formed, another thread can be worked through the centre, twisting the bars to form a twisted border. Fig. 16.4 shows other decorative borders.

Any number of beautiful borders and corners can be

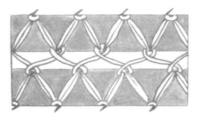

Fig. 16.4a A double border linked with hemstitching.

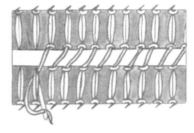

Fig. 16.4b Italian hemstitching.

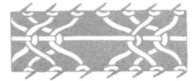

Fig. 16.4c Double twist.

Fig. 16.4d Ladder border.

Fig. 16.4e Bars knotted with coral stitch.

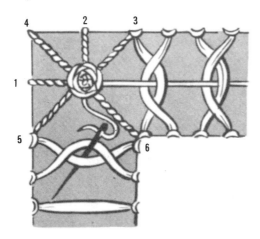

Fig. 16.3 A spider's web corner in drawn threadwork.

Fig. 16.5 Part of a linen table-cloth embroidered in drawn threadwork (dm *Author*).

worked out in drawn threadwork. Scandinavian embroidery books give many of these variations.

Fig. 16.5 shows part of a table-cloth worked in drawn threadwork. The cloth is divided up into squares by simple bar hemstitching. In alternate squares some of the threads are cut and withdrawn, then the square is decorated by drawing these threads together to form the pattern.

17 Embroidery with metallic threads

Metallic threads have been used in embroidery for centuries. Several references are made to them in the Bible. This work too seems to have originated in the East, and it is still widely used there today. Japan, China, India and Turkey produce wonderful embroideries, gold and silver threads being mingled with coloured silks. In India small pieces of mirror are sometimes used as well, surrounded by buttonhole stitches which hold them in place. Fig. 17.1 shows a superb English example from the Elizabethan period.

Today gold work is widely used on church embroideries but this is a very specialised form of work and there are already some excellent books on it. Sometimes, however, a little touch of gold or silver thread may be introduced on an evening bag, evening blouse, slippers, or a jewel box.

A firm foundation is needed for metallic threads, and it

Fig. 17.1 Part of an Elizabethan cover, made of linen (*V & A—crown copyright*).

is often best to have a small piece of fabric as a lining. Use a crewel needle with a fairly large eye so that the thread passes through the fabric easily. For a thin thread there is a choice of suitable stitches, but with a thick thread, couching should be used. If a shaded effect is needed, a silk or a thinner gold or silver thread can be used to couch down the metallic one. If a padded effect is desired, securely overcast several rows of cotton thread, then take the metallic thread over this padding, and hold down each end with a back stitch.

Beads and sequins were lavishly used in Victorian times, on bags, belts, purses, picture frames and cushions. Today they are sometimes used on evening bags or stoles. Individual sequins should be sewn on with a small bead on the top. Stitch through the hole of the sequin, through the bead, then back through the hole of the sequin into the fabric. Groups of overlapping sequins can be sewn on-to a garment, each one having a stitch through the centre which then goes out to the side to take up the next sequin. Fig. 17.3 shows a nylon organza stole embroidered in shadow work with beads and sequins.

Fig. 17.2 *Madonna and Child*, a banner from Chelmsford Cathedral embroidered entirely in gold thread on golden tissue. Some of the embroidery is raised, and in places has been further enriched by the addition of shell jewels (dm *Beryl Dean*).

Fig. 17.3 Beads and sequins are used on this nylon organza stole which is embroidered in close herringbone shadow work (dm *J. E. Andrews, ETC*).

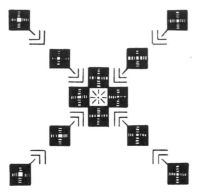

Fig. 18.1 Pattern suitable for Hardanger work. The shaded areas are those from which the threads are withdrawn.

18 Hardanger

This beautiful form of traditional embroidery originated in the little town of Norway from which it takes its name. The peasant women of this mountainous region in the south-west of Norway embroider the most elaborate designs on all kinds of household articles, and on their national costumes, especially on the decorative aprons and blouses. This type of work has now become popular in many other countries and its simplicity is well attuned to modern furnishings. At first the designs were entirely geometrical, but they have been gradually modified and now consist of a combination of grouped blocks of stitches and drawn threadwork. Various patterns, often of darning or surface embroidery, are combined with the geometrical grouped blocks.

The designs can be worked out on graph paper because they consist of diamonds and squares outlined with blocks of satin stitch worked over counted threads. The spaces enclosed by the satin stitchery have the threads cut and withdrawn to form an open space which is afterwards decorated with stitchery patterns, giving a lacy effect. (Fig. 18.1).

The material used for this work should be evenly woven, coarse enough for the threads to be easily counted, and one that does not fray too easily when it is cut. Hardanger canvas is a specially woven, double-thread fabric which is ideal for the purpose. It can be obtained in two thicknesses, but for most work the finer one, which has twenty-two threads to the inch, is the best to use. Fine Glenshee linen can also be used, but it tends to fray a little more. The thread used to overcast the blocks should be slightly thicker than the thread of the fabric, but a finer thread can be used for working the panels of drawn threadwork.

Originally Hardanger work was in white on a white fabric. Today, however, Hardanger canvas is made in several pastel colours and can be worked with a thread of a deeper tone. The most effective work is done on a cream or écru fabric, and embroidered in a deeper cream or natural thread. A No. 23 tapestry needle should be used.

The outlining must be done first. A running stitch should be placed round the blocks and satin stitch worked over this, using an odd number of satin stitches over an even number of threads, usually two, four or six threads. If, for example, four threads are to be withdrawn, five satin stitches will be worked over four threads of the fabric, then four threads are left before starting the next block (Fig. 18.2a). No threads are withdrawn until the parts which will be open have been outlined in this way. When all the squares are complete, the surface embroidery should be worked. Lines can be worked in running stitch, overcasting, square stitch, plaited stitch, and slanting openwork stitch. When all the surface embroidery has been worked a sharp, pointed pair of scissors should be used to cut the threads. They should be cut from the wrong side very close to the satin stitches. Remove the threads in one direction first, then in the other direction. The remaining threads can be made into bars by overcasting or darning them together, or they can be decorated with lace stitches (Fig. 18.2). Bars can either be left plain or decorated with picots. These picots are made on both sides of the bars if no lace stitches are used. Picots in chain stitch are formed of one chain stitch reversed, and worked over the thread with which you are working, and over the loose threads of the web.

Articles worked in Hardanger can be finished with a

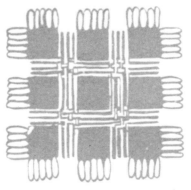

Fig. 18.2a Square with the satin stitch worked and threads withdrawn, leaving only the groups of four threads between the blocks.

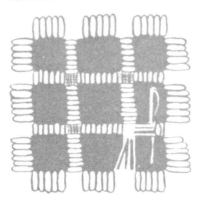

Fig. 18.2b Openwork ground with the bars overcast.

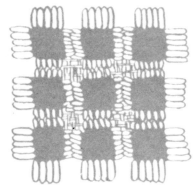

Fig. 18.2c Openwork ground with the bars woven.

[cont. overleaf

Fig. 18.3 Hardanger tray-cloth of cream linen embroidered in natural thread (dm *P. Challenger, ETC*).

Fig. 18.2d Openwork ground with loop stitches set contrariwise, the stitches being worked in vertical rows and alternately, one stitch to the right and one to the left.

small hem and hemstitched, or by very close button-holing around the edge, with the fabric cut away very close up to the buttonholing.

19 Hedebo

Hedebo work is a form of drawn threadwork which originated in Denmark. The correct Danish name is Hedebosyning, the name coming from *Heden*, meaning a heath, and *Bo*, to live.

The Hedebo area west of Copenhagen is famous for its white embroideries (and its gold and silver embroidered women's caps). The peasants embroidered a type of whitework on white, hand-woven linen, which was used to make underclothes, aprons and household articles. In addition, each young girl used to embroider a linen shirt to give as a betrothal gift, in exchange for a carved tool used in the preparation of flax.

The oldest existing pieces date from about 1750, but many of the patterns go back at least to the Renaissance. There are various types, including drawn threadwork borders with filled-in patterns, satin stitch and drawn threadwork used as ornaments only, outlined with tiny, square, cut holes. This early work was purely geometrical in design, and so austere as to be reminiscent of Italian Reticella work. Originally stylised flowers and animals were used, and much of the work looked like lace.

From about 1830 the patterns were drawn fully on the

linen, the outline being chain stitch, and the figures embellished with conventionally treated plants and flowers, filled with different kinds of very fine work. Sometimes satin stitches were also used, as in Fig. 19.1. About 1840 the threadwork becomes more open and filled with patterns in buttonhole stitch, the surroundings being of satin stitch. The floral patterns continue but tend to be freer in style and technique. From about 1850 the material was cut away inside the patterns, and the holes filled with small figures in buttonhole stitch. By the end of the century the designs had become simpler, but stiffer and more formal, as they have remained to this day.

At the beginning of this century architects and artists tried to revive the handicraft from the decline which had set in thirty years earlier, and today it is being taught in the schools, the old patterns and techniques being used for making modern embroideries on articles such as table-mats.

Lace work was used throughout practically the whole period from 1750 to 1850. It consisted of needlelace as edgings for shirts and shifts, and was sewn with buttonhole stitch without any underlying material.

Hedebo work still survives in Denmark, being popular both with amateurs and as a commercial product. Some very old and beautiful pieces of this work can be seen in the Danish Kunstindustri Museum, Copenhagen, and in some British museums. Embroideries somewhat similar to the Hedebo embroideries are found in other parts of Denmark, but they are not so rich or well made.

The white Hedebo embroidery was in former times used for gala shirts and shifts, for bedcovers, ornamental towels, pillowcases and for decorating rooms in the form of hangings over stoves, on cupboards and sometimes

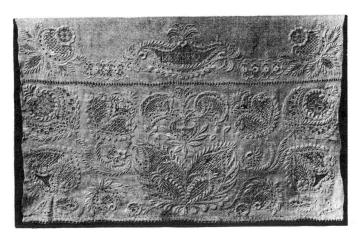

Fig. 19.1 A piece of Hedebo embroidery, 1839. (*DNM*).

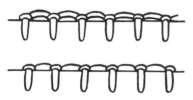

Fig. 19.2a Hedebo buttonholing.

Fig. 19.2b Buttonholed pyramid.

shelves. The coloured embroidery was used for carriage-cushions and women's caps. Today it is still used on towels and household linen, but it is rarely done in any other part of the world than Denmark.

A hand-woven linen is ideal for this work, but sometimes cambric or muslin is used. Usually a whole panel of threads is drawn and decorated, and then a thicker thread is used to weave or darn on the latticed ground. The working thread should be linen and should vary with the thickness of the background. The solid parts are usually embroidered with leaves in satin stitch, and flowers in eyelets similar to Broderie Anglaise. The edges are usually worked in buttonholing, either straight or shaped into scallops or points.

The buttonhole stitch used in Hedebo work is slightly different from the usual one, and is worked from left to right. The stitches should just be far enough apart to allow the knotted edge to lie flat (Fig. 19.2a). The open-work shapes are first outlined with small running stitches, then the fabric is cut and the edges turned back on the wrong side. The edge is then worked with buttonhole stitch. A row of open buttonholing can be worked into the knotted edge, making a stitch between each stitch of the edging (Fig. 19.2b). Crochet and tatting foundations are sometimes used for various lace stitches.

Fig. 20.1 Early seventeenth-century embroidered pillow cover. Silk and metal thread are used on linen; chain, square double-chain, plaited braid, buttonhole and stem stitches are used with couched work (*V & A —crown copyright*).

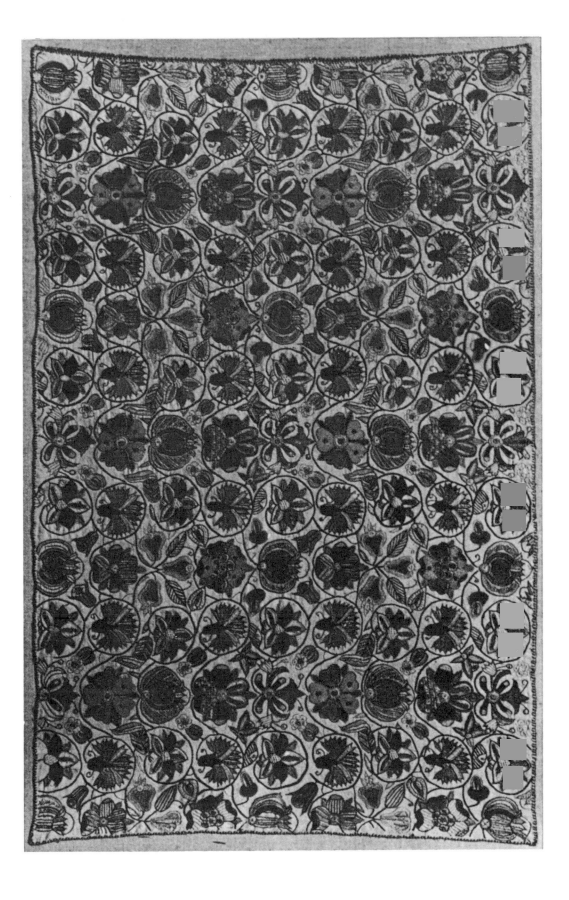

Fig. 20.2 Couching.

20 Laid and couched work

When a number of threads are used on the surface of the material to fill an area the embroidery is called 'laid work'. Fig. 20.1 is a superb example of this work from the early seventeenth century. It is an economical way of using thread as very little goes through to the wrong side, and the right side has a smooth glossy texture. Silk, wool or metallic threads are often used in this way, especially in making church embroideries: If stranded threads are being used, the strands should be untwisted so that they can lie flat. Sometimes the threads used to fix down the silk are invisible, but at other times they form part of the pattern. It is best to lay alternate lines of thread, then come back on a second journey and place another thread between each of the existing ones, each time picking up only a small amount of material. After the whole area has been covered with threads laid in this way, another thread is used to fix these laid threads to the ground, sometimes to form a square or diamond trellis. Couching can also be used to mark the veins of embroidered leaves.

Couching is the name we give to the tying down of threads with small independent stitches. The word comes from the French word *coucher*, meaning to lie down. It is often used as an outline, sometimes with gold or silver thread. Two methods of couching are shown in Fig. 20.2.

21 Machine embroidery

Machine embroidery has in recent years become quite popular. It is exciting to do, and relatively quick, and it lends itself to the simple form of decoration that is particularly suited to modern furniture design. Even with the ordinary domestic sewing machine a number of attractive effects can be obtained, though an electric or treadle machine is necessary, as you will need your hands free to guide the work. Before beginning any piece of work it is wise to practise on a piece of material similar to the one to be used.

In designing for embroidery remember that the machine will give a linear effect only. If solid shapes are to be included in the design a piece of material can be applied. Simple shapes which can be cut in paper should be used (see Fig. 21.1; also Figs. 1.15 and 1.16). Geometrical shapes such as circles, ovals, diamonds and stars are a useful beginning, or you might cut a simple flower or leaf shape in paper, then make up a pattern by adding a few lines with a brush. Next, using the paper pattern, cut out the basic shapes and apply them to the background material by machining around them three or four times and trimming the piece of material back to the outer row of machining. The lines of the pattern can then be drawn on thin paper and machined through, the paper afterwards being torn away, or the lines can be lightly drawn on the fabric with tailor's chalk, a washable pencil or fine water colour paint. These lines can be machined, various thicknesses being obtained by varying the number of rows. If the fabric is very thin, a piece of tissue paper can be placed underneath it, to be torn away on completion.

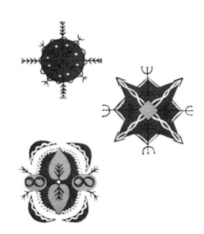

Fig. 21.1 Simple motifs made with cut paper—suitable for machine embroidery.

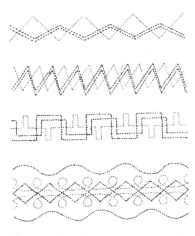

Fig. 21.2 Border patterns for simple machine embroidery.

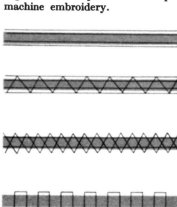

Fig. 21.3 Machined borders using braid or bias binding.

A certain limited amount of embroidery can be done with the presser foot on the machine, but for freer work the foot is removed. No. 40 or No. 50 machine embroidery cotton should be used, together with a No. 11 or No. 14 needle. A good simple beginning can be made by working a few border patterns. Interest can be added by varying the length of the stitch, and the thickness of the thread. Any simple geometrical pattern can be worked in this way. Fig. 21.2 gives some examples. Braids, tapes or wool can be fixed down with decorative machining (Fig. 21.3).

A variation of ordinary machining is known as cable stitch. For this a thicker thread is wound by hand on the bobbin. The bobbin tension thread will probably need loosening to let the thread pass under the tension spring. Using a No. 14 needle and No. 40 cotton, thread up the machine, tighten the top tension and lengthen the stitch. The cable stitch appears on the under side of the work, so be sure to machine on the wrong side. The stitch needs testing to ensure that the tension is right. If the material puckers the under tension is too tight, but if the cable thread loops it is too loose. Wool, silk or even Lurex thread can be used for cable stitch.

Another method of embroidering with the sewing machine is to work appliqué. For quick, bold effects, felt or American cloth are most suitable, as the edges will not fray. Draw the design for the appliqué on a thin piece of paper. Place the felt or fabric to be applied below the background material, and the drawing on top of this. Tack the three layers together. Next machine through the paper, following the lines of the design. This will be the wrong side of the work. When the whole design has been outlined, cut the felt away with a pair of sharp scissors close up to the machining line, leaving the pattern appliquéd on the background. Care should be taken to see that the stitching is not cut.

Shadow appliqué is suitable, too. It is worked in the same way, except that organdie is used and thin materials are applied on the wrong side so that they just show through the organdie.

Designs can be quilted using the quilting foot. A No. 11 needle and No. 50 sewing thread should be used. The pattern is traced on to muslin, which is then tacked to the material with a piece of domette or wadding between the two layers. The pattern is then machined on the wrong side of the work. The tension needs to be adjusted so that the stitch is correct on the right side.

By experimenting you can discover a number of different fillings—zigzag, crazy and granite stitch are shown in Fig. 21.4. A corded effect· can be obtained by using a thick thread on the top, loosening the bottom tension, and slightly loosening the top tension. The bottom thread comes through to the top surface, giving the impression of a whipped cord. A zigzag attachment is useful for working a satin stitch, or for neatening pieces of fabric applied to a picture or wall hanging. For the latter, use a matching thread. For dainty work a few beads or sequins can look well combined with machine embroidery (Fig. 21.5).

Free embroidery work is also possible. Like all machine embroidery this needs to be stretched in a frame, or hoop so that the material lies quite flat. An 8-in. hoop is the best to use. In some machines the feed teeth can be lowered, but if you are using an old machine that is not fitted with a drop feed, you will need to use a cover plate so that the teeth are put out of use. A fine machine needle, e.g. No. 11, should be used with a No. 50 machine embroidery thread. Remove the presser foot, try out the

Fig. 21.4 Various filling stitches which can be done on the ordinary sewing machine.
Zigzag stitch
Crazy stitch
Granite stitch

Fig. 21.5 *Flowers*, a machine-embroidered panel, made of pale pink organdie, with various materials, sequins and beads—all in white, grey and silver—applied (dm *Mary Bryon*).

Fig. 21.6 Net appliqué panel worked on an ordinary sewing machine (dm *Mary Bryon; V & A—crown copyright*).

tension and adjust if necessary. The reverse side of the frame to that used for hand sewing is placed in the machine, the material being flat on the base of the machine. Before beginning work lower the foot lever. Although the presser foot has been removed this is important as it affects the tension. The hoop is held firmly between the thumb and second finger of each hand. It is best not to grip or press on the hoop. Rest your arms on the table and keep the wrists up so that you can get a free movement with the hoop. Draw up the under thread and keeping both threads in the left hand slowly begin to embroider, moving the hoop as you work. It takes quite a lot of practice before you achieve an even rhythm in machine embroidery, moving the hoop slowly to get the effects you desire.

Fascinating pictures and wall hangings can be worked in machine embroidery. Fig. 21.6 shows one in which various fillings have been used most effectively. An appliquéd panel worked in machine embroidery is shown in Fig. 21.7.

22 Mountmellic work

Mountmellic is a single-colour type of embroidery that originated in Ireland. Many years ago a member of the Society of Friends began teaching the Irish peasants how to use this work commercially. It is worked with white thread on white material, and the stitches are grouped to form the design, but unlike other types of white work, no threads are drawn, and there is no cut work.

The designs are simple, bold, and quickly worked. Natural shapes such as leaves, fruits, and flowers are often ˙used, the leaves being filled with a variety of designs similar to those used in Jacobean embroidery. All the floral shapes are treated as naturalistically as possible. Sometimes the flowers are padded with a coarser thread than the one used for the stitchery, and the stems and fruits are also often padded to give a rather bulky effect. Generally surface stitches only are used, but almost any surface embroidery stitch could be employed and interesting fillings evolved. Bullion, feather, thorn, cable, coral and Roumanian stitches, Gordian knots and French knots, are some of the most frequently used.

As this embroidery is heavy a firm material is used, often a thick linen, or a cotton drill.

Mountmellic work is often finished with a buttonholed border, the turreted border being popular. Much of the old work was finished with a knitted fringe.

Fig. 21.7 *Moment Musical*, an appliqué panel (dm *M. Burrows;* *V & A—crown copyright*).

23 Needleweaving

Needleweaving is a very old craft that is known to have been practised for over three thousand years. Fragments of it have been found in the tombs of ancient Egypt. In British museums are treasured several beautiful Coptic fabrics decorated with this work. It is thought that in

Fig. 23.1 Designs for needleweaving.

those days the needle-weaving was worked by hand during the weaving process, while the fabric was still on the loom.

Needleweaving is an attractive form of woven hemstitching, and an enduring version of drawn threadwork. Certain threads are drawn out of the fabric and the weaving is worked over the remaining threads. Narrow borders of this work, done in self-colour, are often known as woven hemstitching. This type of band embroidery can successfully be used on aprons, runners, chair-backs or table linen.

Designs are geometrical and can easily be worked out on graph paper, most designs being based on the square or diamond (Fig. 23.1). Border patterns of zigzag and diagonal lines are often used. Long vertical lines should be avoided as the gaps between the weaving are ugly and during laundering an iron may catch in them and tear the cloth. Vertical lines should be used only when the weaving is done in one colour alone. In this case the threads are pulled tight so that gaps are formed between the blocks of weaving. These gaps supply the interest in this type of work. Monograms can be worked in needleweaving and may be most useful on hand-towels or table napkins. Usually the pattern is formed by changing the colour of the weaving, but occasionally designs can incorporate both blocks of weaving and exposed fabric threads. A border of Holbein work, or simple back stitch can be combined with needleweaving, as the line effect of these will soften the hard outline of the woven border panel (Fig. 23.2).

The fabric used for this type of embroidery needs to be loosely woven with a fairly coarse thread. Almost any good linen crash can be used, but Hardanger, Glamis, Glenshee or huckaback are easy to work on. The threads used should be a little coarser than the weft threads that

Fig. 23.2 Border of a natural chair-back worked in needleweaving and double running in cream, rust and orange Anchor Soft cotton (dm Author).

are withdrawn. Wool, Anchor Soft cotton, *coton-à-broder*, or silk are suitable, each giving a different effect. A blunt tapestry needle should be used, though it is possible to weave with the eye of a needle.

First decide on the position of the panel to be embroidered, then cut the weft threads in the middle and draw them back to the sides of the panel. Each thread should then be darned back for about ¼ in., a process which gives extra strength as well as a neat finish (Fig. 23.3*a*). If a wide border is being worked leave one or two weft threads remaining in the middle of the band. These will later become invisible as they are worked over, but they will help to strengthen the panel. Next the warp threads are grouped into bundles of two or three, by overcasting or hemstitching the top and bottom of the panel (Fig. 23.3*b*). Where a border is to be worked all around a cloth, the threads can be darned back at the corners to leave a square. The buttonholing round these squares will form part of the decoration.

The embroidery consists of weaving over and under these bars or bundles of threads. If a wide elaborate border is being worked it is best to start in the centre and work outwards towards the sides so that the main pattern is exactly central. Begin by darning the thread into the base of the panel, then weave two or three groups of threads together. Go over one group of threads, and under the next, as shown in Fig. 23.4*a*. When one block has been worked, the second one is begun by linking the second and third group of threads together. When a convenient number of blocks in one colour thread have been finished, run the end of the thread into the material and it can be left there until it is needed again. This will save rejoining too frequently. Each block should be tight and firm. This is achieved by constantly pushing the weft

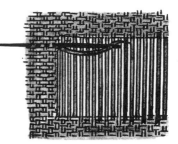

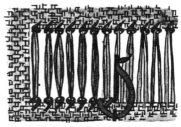

Fig. 23.3 Preparing a needle-weaving border.

Fig. 23.4a Weaving from first block to second.

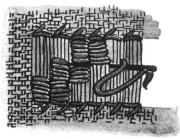

Fig. 23.4b When the top of the threads has been reached, slip the needle down to start the next block.

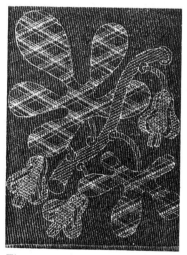

Fig. 24.1 *Fruit*, a panel using white darning on white net, with the simplest of stitchery. The design is derived from a fig tree branch (dm *Emmy Zweybrück-Prochaska; NDS*).

threads together as the needle comes between them. When passing from one block to another, see that the right thread is above the left as this helps to keep the tension even. There should be no gaps between the blocks in coloured needleweaving. Larger blocks can be formed by weaving three or four groups of threads together. When working a zigzag pattern, when the top is reached, slip the needle down to start the next block of weaving, as in Fig. 23.4*b*. Care should be taken to weave the ends of the threads neatly into the bars of weaving, or to darn them in at the top or bottom.

When needleweaving is finished the edges of the border at the sides can be linked to the main material with blanket stitch or overcasting in the colour of the weaving. This will strengthen the work and prevent any gaps being left between the weaving and the fabric.

Great care is needed in pressing needleweaving as it should retain its natural roundness and not be spoilt by flattening. Use a good soft pad and a damp cloth, and press on the wrong side.

24 Net embroidery

Years ago the mesh for this type of work was woven by hand and called 'netting'. Loops of thread were secured by knotting, and formed an open mesh fabric known as *filet* or *lacis*. Later a net canvas called Buratti superseded the material made by this long, slow process. In recent years designs have often been darned on filet net. Sometimes whole articles are made of net, and at other times small panels are inserted into the fabric as decoration. Evening stoles or wedding veils embroider well. Nylon net is best for these.

The design is drawn clearly on paper, and then the net is tacked to this so that the design shows through. The net can have either a square or a hexagonal mesh. Simple shapes, either geometrical or floral, are the best to use (Fig. 24.1). Use a tapestry or blunt-pointed needle so that the mesh is not split.

Start by tying the thread around one strand of mesh, and when it is necessary to join a new thread, knot it to the old one as unobtrusively as possible, as neatness is essential in this type of transparent work. Darning, chain stitch, herringbone or stem stitch can be used or a thread can be couched on the surface.

25 Patchwork

Patchwork consists of the cutting out and sewing together of small pieces of fabric to form a pattern which is also a new, complete article. For centuries women treasured every scrap of cotton, linen, wool or silk and used them to make their patchwork. It is an art that has been practised for thousands of years, probably since the first pieces of simply woven cloth began to wear into holes and to need repairing.

Fig. 24.3 Christening robe made from cotton hexagonal-mesh net. The design is freely drawn, with fillings which range from simple running and darning to complicated Limerick lace patterns. This gives an interesting variety of tones and textures, and the filoselle silk used gives a lovely sheen (dm *Muriel Smith*).

Fig. 24.2 Detail of the embroidery on the christening robe shown in Fig. 24.3.

Fig. 25.1 Patchwork cushion (dm
G. M. Toomey).

Pieces of fabric sewn together to form a design were used by the ancient Egyptians to clothe their kings, and also for their beautiful tent-hangings. One of the oldest extant pieces was made as a pall for the Queen of Egypt some thousand years before the birth of Christ. This piece of work which is now in the Museum in Cairo, consists of a typical Egyptian design of gazelles, scarabs, beetles and lotus flowers. In ancient Greece, China and India, the women made their patchwork into clothes, hangings and covers. In the Middle Ages in Europe beautiful banners were pieced and appliquéd, to be carried into battle.

Throughout the centuries peasants from all over Europe have made patchwork. At first this was done from pure necessity, pieces of old garments being stitched together haphazardly, with no set pattern, to form, in particular, warm bedcoverings. Good fabrics were scarce, and it was an economy, as well as being a decorative way of making covers.

As it developed, patchwork took on a slightly different style in every country. In Britain, it was always closely linked with quilting. When the Pilgrim Fathers went from Holland and England to found the first American colonies, the women took with them this skill of piecing together scraps of fabric to make a pattern, and then quilting it with layers of other materials to keep them warm in the bleak winters. Probably these early settlers in America, thrifty by nature, found life so hard and bleak that to make something that was really beautiful in pattern and colour, with little or no cost, gave them tremendous satisfaction.

Many a family in America still treasures a quilt which was made by a former generation. The Brooklyn Museum, New York, has some exquisite examples of fine workmanship, but few of these go farther back than the beginning of the nineteenth century. One of the most striking things about these old patchwork quilts is their gay and harmonious colour combinations. Amazing, too, is the tremendous patience and neatness which must have been needed. Sometimes as many as sixteen hundred small patches were used on one quilt, all cut on the bias and sewn together so accurately that the whole makes a perfect square.

A few of the quilts made prior to 1800 were over ten feet square, and were made to cover the huge beds which at that time were used by father, mother, and several children. The making of a patchwork quilt was quite a social occasion. Ten or twelve women would meet together and work on one quilt, as modern housewives might meet with their knitting, or to play Bridge. As a girl grew up she would make all the tops which would be stored until such time as she was engaged. Then she would hold 'Quilting Bees', to which her friends would come to help her wad and finish the quilts ready for her new home. A bride would have a chest with a baker's dozen quilts. The thirteenth would be the 'Bridal Quilt', the most elaborate and beautiful of them all, and this last one she would make after her betrothal.

Sometimes a young wife would save a piece from every garment she possessed, beginning with her wedding dress, and add to these pieces from all her children's clothes, together making in one patchwork quilt a record of the family history. Others would make a patchwork for a daughter, collecting a piece from every dress she had, beginning with the christening robe and using a plain cotton patch next to it in the central position, to be replaced later by a piece of white satin from her wedding dress.

Later, 'friendship' quilts were sometimes made. If a

Fig. 25.3 Box pattern, worked in three tones. The darkest piece should always be placed on the same side of the box to form the shadow.

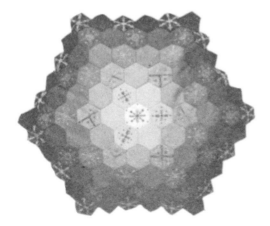

Fig. 25.2 Patchwork cushion made from various shades of blue poplin (dm *A. P. Loveridge, ETC*).

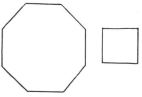

Fig. 25.4 Dutch Tile pattern, made from two shapes, the octagon and the square. If different colours are used for the octagons, four of the same colour should be arranged together. If large shapes are used, a small motif can be embroidered in each octagon.

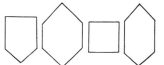

Fig. 25.5 Minton pattern.

woman was leaving a district, each of her friends would contribute a patchwork square; in the centre each donor would write her name in pencil on a plain patch, and then embroider it.

American women made patches in separate squares, then joined these 'blocks' together. The *Rising Sun* or *Sunburst* pattern was one of the most intricate of these block patterns. Different patterns were characteristic of different places, and were often handed down from one generation to the next. The same patterns were sometimes given different names in different districts. For example, *Rambling Road* has been variously called *Indian Trail*, *Flying Dutchman*, *Climbing Rose*, and *Tangled Tares*. Many of the early American pioneers were deeply religious people who had left their home countries because of their faith. It is not surprising therefore that many of the patterns were given names associated with the Scriptures, such as *The Crown of Thorns*, *Jacob's Ladder*, *Joseph's Coat*, *Hosanna*, *Star of Bethlehem*, and *King David's Crown*. Other names such as *Indian Meadow*, *Texas Rose*, *Rocky Road to Kansas*, and *Road to California*, were connected with the newly discovered country. Fig. 25.1 shows one of these traditional American pattern's, *Philadelphia Pavement*, made from *Shoo-fly* (centre) with printed border.

The earliest type of patchwork in this country is believed by some to have been crazy patchwork. Every scrap of material can be used in this work as each piece can be a different shape and size. Any type of material can be used and sometimes wool, cotton, and silk are found together. All the pieces are sewn onto a foundation, and often the seams are covered with an embroidery stitch such as feather stitch, or herringbone.

Many references to patchwork are to be found in

household lists of the seventeenth century, but the greatest period for this craft was between about 1795 and 1870.

Mosaic patchwork is the original type of patchwork and the method of joining the pieces to each other has changed very little in the centuries. Pieces of work judged to have been done in the sixth and ninth centuries were found some years ago when archaeological surveys were being made in caves beyond the Ganges. One of these pieces, a silk hanging, was made of pieces of silk and damask, probably pieces left by travellers at a shrine, who might have torn them off their clothes. The method used to oversew these patches was very similar to that used today.

In all forms of patchwork good designs depend on careful thought and planning, so that the arrangement of the pieces display colour and tone to their best advantage. Sometimes inspiration can be gained from mosaics, Roman pavements, or designs of similar geometrical shape. It is usually helpful to place the pieces in different positions, pinned to a piece of cork, and experiment until you get a successful arrangement. Figs. 25.3 to 25.9 show possible designs.

Different shades of the same colour are attractive, or plain and patterned materials can be used together. Fig. 25.2 shows a cushion made from various shades of blue poplin. The pieces are shaded from white in the centre to navy blue on the outside. Stripes, checks, and spots in different combinations make interesting patterns. The careful distribution of colours, both tones and contrasts, is most important. Use more plain than printed fabrics, or the design will become restless.

In working patchwork, you should never mix materials that will not launder with those that launder easily. For

Fig. 25.6 Trellis pattern, using two shapes. These can be in two shades of the same colour or in a light and a dark colour.

Fig. 25.7 Star pattern, effective with two materials of different textures and colour. The squares could be in a third material, or plain if the star were patterned.

Fig. 25.8 Sixteen-pointed star.

Fig. 25.10 Template frame used for centring the fabric.

this reason, never mix cotton and rayon or cotton and silk, though silk and velvet are occasionally used together. It is also best to avoid having too many textures in the same piece of work. It is really better to use the same type of fabric throughout, simply varying the size and shape of the patches. To join them you will want a No. 80 or No. 100 thread to match the main colour of the patches, and a very fine needle.

Hexagons, squares, diamonds, triangles, octagons, lozenges, stars, crescents and rectangles are some of the shapes used for patches. Long diamonds, long hexagons, and long octagons are also common. Templates for these can be drawn out on card and cut very accurately, though today metal or plastic ones are available. It is useful to have a mask to go with each template which can be used as a guide when you cut out your pieces of patterned fabric. The mask is ¼ in. larger all round than the template, which allows for the turning on the patch, and the hole in the middle of it enables you to position flowers or parts of a printed pattern (Fig. 25.10).

When you have decided which templates you want to use, paper shapes need to be cut for each patch. It is most important that these should be absolutely accurate, pieces of similar shapes being identical. Thick note-paper can be used, and the paper that is used for Annual Company Reports is excellent. In the past women are said to have used their love letters, and in some of the old quilts the papers were left in after the quilt was finished. This no doubt gave extra warmth, but quilts of this kind could not be washed. Card can be used if preferred, but it needs to be very thin. The metal or plastic templates can be placed on top of two layers of paper (never cut more than two shapes at once), and cut round with sharp scissors, or a razor blade. One old lady,

Fig. 25.9 Sixteen-pointed star.

who did most beautiful patchwork, always used news-paper, and folded it over the template; she then slipped the template out leaving the folded newspaper to be used for the patches. Whichever method is used it is essential that the papers are cut accurately. If you are going to make a very large piece of work such as a quilt, the papers can be used several times to save the labour of cutting every piece.

The patches are then cut, leaving $\frac{1}{2}$ to $\frac{1}{4}$ in. turnings. Use an iron to press the turnings over the paper, then tack each patch as shown in Fig. 25.11d. It is a help to mark on the template the way of the grain of the fabric so that the warp of all the pieces runs the same way. This is vital with large pieces, but for those with a diameter of 1 in. or under it is not quite so important, and sometimes with a striped or patterned material it may be necessary to use some of the patches on the cross to obtain an interesting effect.

When all the patches have been tacked to the papers, arrange them to form the pattern, and begin joining them. Place the right sides together and overcast the edges using very small stitches on the wrong side. Take up only one or two threads of the fabric in each stitch. When any patch has been completely surrounded, the paper can be removed, and used again if necessary. When all tacking threads have been removed, press all the seams on the wrong side.

If decorative stitchery, such as herringbone or feather stitch, is added on the right side to cover the joins, the thread should be of a light neutral colour which will tone with all the colours used in the work.

Patchwork always needs a lining. If warmth is needed an interlining of wool or wadding can be used, and a little quilting added to keep the layers firmly together.

Fig. 25.11a Metal templates of a hexagon and a diamond are obtainable from the Embroiderers' Guild in the size shown here, as well as in a size larger and a size smaller.

Fig. 25.11b Place the template on paper; cut round it.

Fig. 25.11c Place paper template on fabric, and cut out, leaving $\frac{1}{4}$ in. turnings.

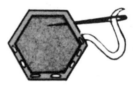

Fig. 25.11d Press turnings of fabric over paper and tack down.

Fig. 25.12a Template for shell or scale patchwork.

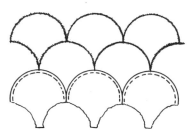

Fig. 25.12b Top two rows of scales have been hemmed down on the right side, and the third row is tacked in position ready to be hemmed.

Fig. 25.13 Apron decorated with applied patchwork. Plain blue denim was used for the apron, a darker blue, a check, and spot fabric for the patchwork (dm *Author*).

Nowadays coverlets are more usual; these have a cotton lining, but no wadding or quilting. A plain border is most suitable for a patchwork coverlet.

Shell or scale patchwork is unlike mosaic patchwork in that the pieces are joined on the right side. This template is used as an all-over pattern. The pieces are cut as for mosaic patchwork, but instead of the fabric being tacked over the paper, the top edge is carefully turned down on the wrong side. It is best to place the template on the right side of the fabric, then carefully turn this down onto the wrong side, making very small pleats as you go around the curved edge. This turning is then tacked down. When all the shells are prepared in this way, pin them on a piece of cork, one row at a time. Accurate placing is essential. Next hem down the top edges one row at a time. Each scale overlaps the row above, as in Fig. 25.12*b*. An interesting diagonal effect is achieved by using alternate light and dark patches. This pattern is not often used, and more skill in joining the patches is necessary than for mosaic patchwork.

Applied or appliquéd patchwork can, if carefully planned, be most effective. Sometimes templates are used, as for mosaic patchwork; at others the shapes are cut freely, joined and applied. In this work the whole is not made up of pieces; the patchwork is used instead to decorate a piece of fabric. Fig. 25.13 shows an apron decorated with the traditional pattern called *The Ocean Wave*.

Log cabin or Canadian patchwork differs from mosaic patchwork in that the pieces are cut in strips, and then run one on top of the other from the centre, being turned down so that no stitches are allowed to show. This type of patchwork is often known as log-house quilting. All the strips are equal in width but of different lengths— each one from the centre being a little longer than the

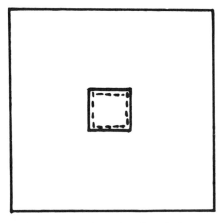

Fig. 25.14a A 7 in. foundation square with the 1¼ in. square tacked in the middle.

previous one. Usually the design is made in two shades, a light and a dark.

Use a foundation square of side 7 in., cut a square of light coloured material of side $1\frac{1}{4}$ in., then cut two light and two darker strips each 1 in. wide and $1\frac{1}{2}$ in. long. Tack the light square in the centre of the foundation square. Fold the first strip in half lengthways, and place the fold just over the raw edge of one side of the square. Run through the middle of this strip on the fold line, then fold it down to make a strip $\frac{1}{2}$ in. wide with the stitches hidden in the fold. The next strip is then placed on the second side of the square the fold overlapping the raw edge. This is run through the middle and turned down in the same way. Continue going around the square in this way, each new strip just overlapping the one above it.

This is very effective for a cushion or coverlet. Make the necessary number of squares, then join them together.

26 Pulled or drawn fabric work

This type of work should not be confused with drawn threadwork, as the threads of the fabric are not withdrawn. Instead the stitches are worked in such a way that the threads are 'drawn' together or 'pulled' aside to leave holes and openwork patterns. It is a very old form of embroidery and some beautiful work has been done in places as far apart as the Greek Islands, India, and

Fig. 25.14b The first strip is tacked over the square with the fold slightly overlapping the raw edges.

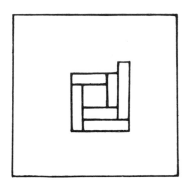

Fig. 25.14c Several strips have been stitched down, each overlapping the previous one.

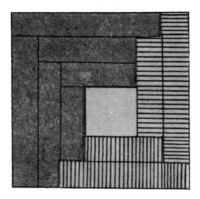

Fig. 25.14d Showing how light and dark fabric can be used for opposite sides of the square.

Fig. 26.1 Corner of a tray-cloth embroidered in natural thread pulled work on natural Danish net. Four-sided stitch and satin stitch have been used to form the pattern (dm *D. P. Wood, ETC*).

Fig. 26.2 Lid and one side of a trinket box of blue Danish net embroidered in white thread in pulled stitches and satin stitch (dm *Hazel Bower, ETC*).

Scandinavia. In the seventeenth and eighteenth centuries, much of it was done in Germany, Denmark, and Flanders, and some of the most beautiful results there resembled needlepoint lace. Dresden work (Fig. 9.1), sometimes known as Saxony lace, became world famous. Various pulled stitches formed the designs which were worked on very fine cambric and used to decorate shirts, blouses, and underclothes, and also worked on heavier, coarser fabric for waistcoats, bedhangings, and curtains. The earliest Ayrshire embroidery evolved from this Dresden work. Much of this exquisite embroidery was done on the sheerest lawns and looked like fine lace; muslin, too, was flowered with delicate pulled work. Some lovely examples are to be seen in the Victoria and Albert Museum.

Today the work has been revived and is popular in Germany and the Scandinavian countries. It can successfully be used to decorate table-mats, table-cloths, tray-cloths and similar articles.

There are a vast number of stitches and each country has its own favourites. Each stitch forms its own pattern, which is usually used as a filling or in a geometrical shape (Fig. 26.1). If the stitches are to be used as fillings the design should be simple with bold outlines (Fig. 26.3).

Easy patterns for pulled work can be built up by cutting out leaf shapes in paper, and arranging them to form a pattern. These shapes can be given bold outlines, filled with pulled work and linked with a few simple lines. All the stitches are worked on counted threads, and their size can be varied according to the fabric. Diagonal raised band, four-sided stitch, honeycomb, rosette, Greek Cross, mosaic, and oblique fillings are some of the most commonly used stitches.

Material for drawn fabric work should be even-weave linen, which is obtainable in various weights. A fine

Fig. 26.3 Square cloth from Sweden. Cream linen with a geometrical pattern in white (*NDS*).

linen or scrim will give a lacy effect, whereas a heavier Glenshee or Glamis will have different uses. Lauder gauze scrim, and Bisso linen are both easy to work on and suitable for fine work. Danish net is finer still and very attractive, the pale blue being especially beautiful (Fig. 26.2). Linen of white or natural is most common, but it is possible to work with a white thread on a pale blue, grey, or green.

A hard linen thread should be used, the thickness varying with the fabric and the size of the stitch. It should be a little thinner than the threads of the background fabric though a thicker thread can be used for surface stitches and outlines. It is best to use a short length of linen thread, about fifteen to eighteen inches. One sharp pull is then given to each stitch and it is possible to get an even rhythm and a good tension. The tension of the stitch is one of the most important details in pulled work; the whole effect is spoilt if this is irregular.

The thread should always be the same hue as the linen, but it can be just a shade darker or lighter. Knox's Linen Lace thread is obtainable in various shades of cream and natural, and No. 50 is a good thread for medium weight Glamis linen. D.M.C. Lace threads are excellent, but are made in only two shades.

A blunt-pointed tapestry needle should be used and the thread should frequently be moved in the eye of the needle as linen easily wears rough, and this spoils the appearance of the work. Hold the work the way the stitches will travel; this will make it easier to keep the tension even. Always work below the previous row even if it means fastening off and restarting again. It is useful to work with a dark cloth on your lap so that the holes will show up and any mistake will be readily seen.

Fig. 26.4b Detail of the tray-cloth.

Fig. 26.4a Tray-cloth embroidered in a simple geometrical border of pulled work (dm *J. Round, ETC*).

Fig. 26.5 Three of a set of table-mats of Glenshee linen embroidered with various pulled work stitches in a natural linen thread (dm *Author*).

If you have not done any of this work before it is best to begin on a small mat or tray-cloth that will not take too long to do. Decide on the approximate size and shape of the article and tack around it. Do not make a hem until the work is finished. If a border is to be worked, start in the middle and work out so as to make the corners identical. Simple geometrical designs are good for beginners (Fig. 26.4). Draw the design on the fabric, then fill in the various shapes with two or three different stitches. Care must be taken in finishing off stitches. At the end of a row the finishing off has often to be adjusted so that it produces the correct 'pull'. The threads can be taken along the back to a spot just past where the needle should emerge.

If a line is to be whipped, each stitch should be made with a straight sharp pull upwards, to be sure the holes are even. Satin stitch fillings combine well with pulled work. The outlines of the pattern can be worked after the fillings are completed. Whipped and threaded stitches such as Portuguese border, coral, raised stem, raised chain, or close herringbone stitch can well be used for outlining.

When the embroidery is completed, the work should be stretched. A coarse braid can be machine-tacked to the edges of the fabric, then pinned out on damp blotting paper and left to dry. After stretching, the hems should be worked. These should be as narrow as possible, and can be finished with four-sided stitch, or hemstitching.

Fig. 26.5 shows three of a set of table-mats, each embroidered with a different pattern of pulled work. This would be an ideal way for a beginner to start on this type of work, as the mats can act as samplers of the various stitches.

27 Quilting

Quilting is a decorative method of sewing together two or three layers of fabric. The word 'quilt' comes from the French word *cuilte*, which was derived from the Latin word *culcita* meaning a stuffed sack or cushion. Sometimes the word was spelt *cowltes* or *qwhiltez*. It was originally used to produce warm clothing and bedcovers. An old blanket and sheet would be put by, together with pieces of old dresses which would be patched together. The three layers could then be quilted to make a warm covering costing little or nothing. At first the stitchery was purely utilitarian, its purpose being simply to hold the layers firmly together, but soon it was found that by following simple patterns the stitchery could form a beautiful design.

Quilting is a very ancient craft which was used even in primitive times. There is little information about the early history of quilting, but some of the pictures in old Egyptian friezes show garments that look as if they were quilted. The Normans are known to have worn a quilted garment as part of their armour. The knights wore it under their hauberk, but some of the ordinary soldiers wore it as an external protection. Specimens of thirteenth-century work have been found in various parts of the world. The quilted surcoat of the Black Prince is still preserved in Canterbury Cathedral. Throughout the Middle Ages it was the custom for soldiers to wear quilted garments beneath their armour to prevent it chafing. No doubt in peace time too quilted clothes gave warmth in the cold, draughty castles. Later, in Tudor times doublets and petticoats were quilted. Towards the end of

Fig. 27.1a Welsh quilt made in 1933. (*V & A—crown copyright*).

the eighteenth century, Queen Anne did some most beautiful work which is still in existence today. In the seventeenth century the art of quilting was carried to America by the settlers who used it with their patchwork. The huge quilts were often communal efforts, several women joining together to quilt the patchwork 'tops' which had previously been pieced together.

Fig. 27.1*b* shows part of a coverlet made in the first half of the eighteenth century. It was made of linen, quilted with yellow silk in back stitch.

By the end of the eighteenth century quilted garments were no longer fashionable, but for another hundred years quilting was practised by the country folk, especially in more remote places where it was not easy to get things from the shops. By this time 'marcella' quilts were being made in the factories. These were white cotton coverlets woven to imitate quilting. They soon became fashionable in the towns, but were not as warm as the handmade quilts of the country, which continued to be made until as recently as the beginning of this century in parts of Devon and Cornwall, as well as in Northumberland, Cumberland, Durham, and Wales.

Women in Durham and Wales found that their quilting was more effective if worked on plain white, or pale-coloured fabric, rather than patterned cotton and in these parts, late in the nineteenth century, quilting became divorced from patchwork. Many farmhouses in remote parts still treasure their handsewn quilts. Welsh fishermen's wives, and women who worked in the fields of Northumberland, wore thickly quilted petticoats or voluminous skirts to keep them warm. Every farmhouse had its quilting frame, and Welsh and Durham women can still recall threading the needles for the older women to quilt, when they themselves were far too young to join

Fig. 27.1b English quilting of the
early eighteenth century (*V & A—
crown copyright*).

Fig. 27.2a *(See below.)*

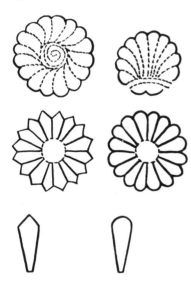

Fig. 27.2b Some traditional quilting designs.

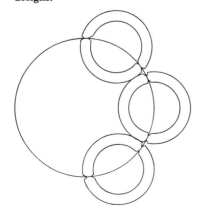

in the work. A spell at the quilting frame was a regular part of the day's work, and sometimes even the men played their part, drawing the patterns on the stone floor of the farmhouse kitchen, or making the templates from wood or tin. Often several neighbours would join together to help one another, making quilts for each family in turn.

Both in Durham and South Wales there were professional quilters. These women took orders for quilts from people in all the surrounding villages. Many people could do patchwork, but the really skilled quilter was more rare. It was an art which needed great dexterity with both hands. The most competent of them worked equally well with each hand but others never became expert at this. Taking small, even stitches through three layers of fabric often made the needle bend, and a bent needle was treasured, as it was the better suited to dainty work. Some of these women were not only skilled craftswomen, but also real artists. Many of the old quilts had most intricate designs and were as beautiful on the wrong side as the right. They worked from morning to night; some of the quicker ones made as many as two quilts in a week, while others took a fortnight to make one. A great deal depended on how much fine stitchery was used on the quilt.

Quilting patterns were sometimes bought, printed on thin paper, and a tracing wheel was used to transfer them to the right side of the work. Towards the end of the nineteenth century, indeed, women's magazines and newspapers printed quilting designs. The professional quilter however usually made up her own designs or used those that had been handed down through generations.

Usually customers bought their own materials, and paid about five shillings to have them made up. In the North

Fig. 27.2c If the circular template is to be used to make a ring, chalk a large circle to pass through the centres of the templates, snipping a notch in the middle of each so that this can be matched exactly on the circumference of the circle.

Fig. 27.2a Templates for quilting. Circles can be drawn with compasses, a cup, saucer, or plate. Continuous lines indicate the outline and dotted lines are added in freehand for sewing. Circles can be linked or overlapping, especially when used as a border pattern. A line is used as a guide. The overlap is marked by small notches on the edge of template. This template can also be used on a perpendicular or a diagonal axis. One template can be made for use with various patterns. Fold a circle across its centre into any number of segments and cut for points or scallops, and for a hole in the centre. The latter is always included to avoid too many lines all meeting at a point. Unfold and you will have a template which can be filled in various ways.

there were professional 'stampers', or pattern markers. Some of these were not actually quilters themselves, but they designed and marked out quilts for the women to work. From 1860 to 1900 there were also travelling quilters who went from farm to farm, sometimes staying as long as two weeks to quilt and dressmake. These quilters were given their food and anything from sixpence to one shilling a day for their work.

In the mining villages of South Wales, quilting clubs were started towards the end of the nineteenth century, and a few are still in existence. Fig. 27.1*a* shows a quilt made at Porth Rhondda, in 1933. Often these clubs were started by widows who wanted to earn a living. Wages were very low at that time, and few people could afford to buy the materials for a quilt, while the quilter could not afford to buy them herself, or to wait weeks before she was paid for her work. When the miners got their wages a shilling would therefore be paid into the club, so that the quilter was able to earn a reasonable living by making quilts for all the members. In the North many chapels had their own quilt clubs, groups of women working together to raise money for their chapel, and these continued until the Second World War, when fabrics were rationed for the first time.

English quilting designs are planned by using templates which are arranged on the fabric and marked round with a needle (Fig. 27.2). A tapestry or blunt-pointed needle should be used for marking. It is held almost flat so that the material is creased but not scratched.

Many traditional designs have been handed down from mother to daughter, and are given names which vary from district to district. Fig. 27.2 shows a few of these, namely *The Rose*, *The Shell*, and *The Star*. As the quilting design should be planned to fill the whole space, a main

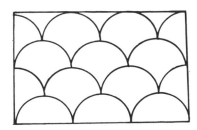

Fig. 27.2d Design using scale template.

Fig. 27.2e Design using petal template.

Fig. 27.2f Design using cable template.

Fig. 27.3a Feather design for quilting.

Fig. 27.3b Feather pattern quilted on a crêpe-de-chine bedjacket.

pattern can be used, with an all-over pattern for the background. The stitches hold the padding in place, and no area measuring more than two inches across should be left unquilted. In addition to the needle-marking around the templates, which gives the outline of the pattern, tailor's chalk can be used for some parts of the pattern as this can be brushed off when the work is finished. Shapes for the pattern need to be simple and effective. Templates are often circles, scales, lozenges, cables, diamonds, triangles, squares, hexagons, petals, ellipses, or feathers. Backgrounds of interlaced circles, squares, or diamonds are effective. A diamond check pattern is known as 'gamboised'. Household articles such as cups and plates are often used as a basis for the templates, while others are obtained by simply folding and cutting paper shapes (Fig. 27.2). The actual templates are made of cardboard, plywood, or metal. 'Mill-net', which was an open mesh material stiffened with glue and starch, was sometimes used by the old quilters.

Materials for quilting should be soft and smooth, closely woven with a slightly lustrous, but not too shiny, surface. Silk, poplin, crêpe-de-chine, or dull satin are suitable. Fine linen was frequently used in the past. Material of any colour can be used, but lighter colours give a better effect. If a lining is to be used, it can be a contrasting colour, otherwise the bottom layer can be of sheeting or muslin. Wadding, domett, or old blankets will do for the middle layer of padding. Sheep's wool, or fleece, carefully washed to remove grease, can also be used successfully. If cotton-wool or wadding is used it should be of good quality; medicated cotton wool should not be used.

Quilting should be worked on a frame, and can be made reversible, the stitches being taken through both layers of fabric and the layer of wadding which is between them.

A quilting frame consists of four strips of wood with a braid along the inner edge. The work is tacked to the braid. For smaller pieces of work an ordinary embroidery frame can be used.

The three layers of material are arranged with the lining or muslin first, next the padding, then the upper layer. These three layers are tacked together in all directions to prevent them moving. It is best to start tacking in the middle and constantly smooth out the material, stitching out to each side, and diagonally to each corner. Next find the exact centre and mark it with a pin. A template can then be used, and the design needlemarked on the top layer of fabric. Back stitch, running stitch or chain stitch can be used for outlining the pattern, but only one stitch should be used throughout. If chain stitch is used it should be worked from the back, leaving an unbroken line of back stitches on the front. Every stitch must be made in two movements, upwards and downwards, going through all three layers of fabric. Each stitch should be as regular and even as possible, but it need not be too small. Begin with a knot that is pulled through the lower layer.

When the work is finished remove all the tacking stitches and neaten the edges. A corded edge makes a good finish. Another method is to turn in both edges and run a line of stitching as near to the edge as possible and a second line $\frac{1}{8}$ to $\frac{1}{4}$ in. farther in. Edges should never be finished by machine stitching.

Italian or corded quilting. This is a purely decorative form of quilting, used for cushions, tea-cosies, bedjackets, slippers, cotcovers or nightdress cases (Fig. 27.5). Two layers only are used—a muslin backing to the top fabric. The design is stamped, or pounced onto the under muslin, and this is then securely tacked to the top fabric.

Fig. 27.4 English quilting showing the rosette and feather used in a design (*V & A—crown copyright*).

Fig. 27.5 Quilted night-dress case, worked mainly in Italian quilting, combined with a little Trapunto (m *A. P. Loveridge, ETC*).

Fig. 27.6 Corded quilting—part of a linen robe, late seventeenth century (*V & A—crown copyright*).

The design is outlined from the wrong side with a double row of small running stitches, worked through both layers, and about $\frac{1}{8}$ to $\frac{1}{4}$ in. apart. A cord or length of thick wool is threaded from the back through the muslin, throwing the outline of the design into relief. Interlaced lines and Celtic patterns lend themselves to this type of work of which Fig. 27.6 is an exquisite example.

The 'lining' or 'padding' is added after the work is finished. Use thick wool, slip the needle through the muslin, between the two layers and through the double outline around the pattern. When there is a sharp curve or angle bring the needle out and insert it again through the same hole, or a little farther along, and continue threading, leaving the loose wool at the angle to form a small loop. This will prevent the padding pulling or shrinking when it is washed.

Shadow quilting. This is a variation of Italian or corded quilting. A thin transparent material is used, such as silk or organdie, and the wool used for padding is brightly coloured so that it shows through the upper layer giving a 'shadow' effect. Sometimes cut work designs can be adapted for Italian or shadow quilting, as these designs always have a double outline. The work can be pressed when it is finished by covering it with a cloth and using the tip of the iron on the areas between the corded lines. A well padded ironing cloth or small pad will help.

Trapunto is another form of quilting, again through two layers—the top fabric and a layer of muslin. It is most commonly used for cushions or cotcovers. The design is drawn on the muslin before it is tacked securely to the top layer. The design is a single outline which is stitched from the back through the two layers. Cotton wadding is then drawn through the muslin from the back with a

Fig. 27.7 Cushions: corded linen quilting; English quilting in tussore silk (dm *D. P. Lyster, R. A. Burtt; FWI*).

crochet hook, so that flowers or leaves are padded. Small shapes are best as these can be padded evenly. The finished result is a pattern in relief.

28 Renaissance, Richelieu and Reticella work

These three types of embroidery are all variations of cut work. Cut work can be seen on many early English samplers, but it probably originated in Italy, since many sixteenth-century pattern books contained designs for this type of work. It is sometimes called Venetian embroidery because it resembles Venetian lace, the linen corresponding to the needle-made ground of the lace.

It is used to decorate table linen and bed linen, and handkerchiefs.

Designs for this work must be simple and bold, the shapes and motifs overlapping each other so that the spaces between can be cut away, leaving the design linked in certain places (Fig. 28.1).

Finely woven linen or cotton is the best material to use as it will not fray too much. The threads should usually be similar in thickness to the ground, and if not the same colour, only a shade lighter or darker.

Care must be taken to see that when the work is cut, no part of the design will be loose. The parts that are cut away should be quite small so that there is no danger of an iron catching in the holes. Two rows of small running stitches should first be worked around the whole design.

These running stitches can then be covered with close overcasting, using a very fine needle. Edges can also be buttonholed, but here, too, the running stitches are done before the buttonholing is worked over them, with each stitch touching the previous one. The knotted part of the stitches comes on the edge that is to be cut away. Great care is needed in cutting away the fabric very close to this edge. An extremely sharp pair of scissors with curved points will be useful as the cutting needs to be precise and accurate. A looped edge is still more firm than a buttonholed one; it is often used when fillings are to be worked into it. Sometimes the outlines are padded by couching cotton along the edge before working the stitching over it. Raised, padded dots are often used with this type of work, and sometimes filling stitches and lace stitches are also combined with it.

If a very fine fabric is being used the open areas can be cut in such a way that the points of the fabric are caught back underneath the stitching. They are cut away on the wrong side after the stitching back is completed. The edge is then a fold, and will wash and wear longer than a cut edge.

Renaissance work is another type of cut work, but the areas of open work are larger and bars are introduced to link the spaces. These bars are the main characteristic of this work. The threads on which the bars are embroidered are sewn from side to side of the space at the time when the running stitches are being worked. A bar usually consists of three or four threads which are worked with buttonhole stitch or weaving before the main shapes are outlined with buttonhole stitch. Great care is needed in cutting the fabric in Renaissance work as the bars have to remain when the material beneath them has been cut away.

Fig. 28.1 Design for cut work showing how the shapes overlap to leave the design firm when the small background pieces are cut away.

Richelieu work is very similar to Renaissance work—the spaces are linked with bars, but the bars are more decorative. Most of the bars are embroidered with picots and this gives an even richer appearance to the finished article.

Reticella work is yet another form of cut work and one which resembles Reticella lace. This work was largely done from about 1480 to 1620, when needlepoint took its place. In the late sixteenth century it was most popular and many pattern books were published to encourage its practice. It was often used for cuffs and ruffs. Today it is still done at Torcello, near Venice.

A panel or circle of fabric is cut away and the space delicately worked. The material is first tacked to a piece of stiff paper or cloth so that the threads keep straight. The decoration is usually geometrical, using bullion and other raised stitches. The embroidery around the cut work is important; small shapes are cut away and then worked with simple fillings.

29 Shadow work

Shadow work is probably of Indian origin, but it first became popular in England in the eighteenth century. It was always worked on fine white fabric and consisted of stitching worked on the wrong side of transparent fabric so that a shadow effect was produced on the right side.

This type of work is very effective for lingerie, babies'

Fig. 29.1 Simple designs suitable for shadow work, using close herringbone.

Fig. 29.2 Central design of a table-cloth embroidered in white and coral shadow work (m *D. Holdaway, ETC*).

Fig. 29.3 Designs for block shadow work.

dresses, babies' pillowcases, duchess sets, table-mats, tray-cloths, table-cloths, tea-cosies or lampshades.

Organdie, muslin, nylon, or fine linen lawn or scrim are suitable, especially if worked with simple floral designs (Fig. 29.1). Today colours are often used for shadow work although white is very effective.

There are several varieties of shadow work.

Block shadow work is often used on lingerie, or blouses. It is extremely dainty and can be worked on muslin, voile, organdie, or thin silk or rayon. The design can be traced by placing the fabric over it and outlining it with a pencil or small paint brush. The stitchery is usually executed with white or coloured thread—for example, one strand of pure silk Filoselle or one thread of stranded cotton. Close herringbone is worked on the wrong side in one direction, then another row is worked at right angles to, and on top of, the first. Squares, diamonds, or simple shapes can be worked in this way. Simple designs for block shadow work are shown in Fig. 29.3.

Close herringbone is used for comparatively small areas of shadow work. Unlike the method used for block shadow work, the herringboning is worked only one way across the shape. In larger spaces it is sometimes best to work in two halves. (For example, the top part of a leaf can be worked in two halves, the two lines left in the centre representing the central vein of the leaf.) Whenever close herringbone is used two lines of back stitch are formed on the right side and these outline the design. Occasionally an extra stitch or two is necessary to ensure that the outline is continuous. Single lines in a design are worked with back stitch on the right side of the material, or stem stitch may be used if preferred. Fig. 29.4 shows some table-mats worked in this way.

Indian shadow work is a slightly different method,

Fig. 29.4 *Sea Shells* table-mats in white organdie (d *Lana Mackinnon,* m *Jessie Dunn; CoID*).

though the final effect is similar. The stitches do not cross, as in herringbone, but zigzag from side to side. Only very little material should be picked up at each stitch, otherwise the threads will be too open at the back and the shadow effect on the right side will be spoilt.

In both these types of embroidery the stitches need to be very even, but on a curve they should vary in size; on the outer curve the stitches will be slightly larger than on the inner curve.

Shadow appliqué, too, is worked on transparent fabrics such as organdie or lawn, and is a method which can be used if the work is to be backed with a lining. Small pieces of coloured fabric are tacked on the wrong side of the work and the design is outlined with very fine chain stitch or pin stitch. The applied fabric is then cut away from the back, leaving the design appliquéd on the wrong side and showing through to the right side as a shadow. Surface stitchery can then be worked on the right side. This method is especially suitable for table-cloths where areas of design may be relatively large. It can be combined with close herringbone work on the smaller parts of the design. Fig. 29.5 gives the outline of a tea-cosy design for working in this way, and Fig. 29.6 illustrates the finished article.

Fig. 29.5 Design for a tea-cosy in shadow appliqué.

Fig. 29.6 The same tea-cosy with surface embroidery to give texture to the leaves (dm *Author*).

Fig. 30.1a Long and short edge.

Fig. 30.1b Split stitch.

30 Silk embroidery

For centuries this work has been done in various parts of the world, but it originated, and some of the best examples of it have been done, in the Far East, perhaps because the most exquisite silks are so plentiful there. Shading in silk embroidery is like painting, and the aim in this work is to make natural forms look as lifelike as possible. Fig. 30.2 shows a piece of English early eighteenth-century work. At this period it was at the height of its popularity and some beautiful work was done. Today, however, it is not in fashion, and little is done in this country. The frontispiece shows an embroidered picture from this same period; in it the long and short stitch can be clearly seen.

Before beginning this type of work it is essential to study plant forms and make colour sketches of them, noticing the range of colour and shadow. Study the whole plants, the joints, the leaves, and the direction of the growth. Great care is always necessary in placing the light and shade. The direction of stitch is one of the most important factors in this work.

The background is usually firm silk or satin, but a dull mat-surfaced fabric gives the best effect. Filoselle is a good choice for the stitchery, as there is a wide choice of colour, and the number of strands can be varied. A frame is needed—a tambour frame—and both hands should be used. Around the edge of the leaf or flower work a long and short stitch, then in the second row, bring the needle up half way through the stitches in the previous row; all the stitches are the same length, but alternate so that they look like long and short stitches.

Fig. 30.2 Early eighteenth-century apron in silk embroidery (V & A—crown copyright).

Another way to make a smooth edge is to use split stitch. These are all shown in Figs. 30.1*a*, *b* and *c*.

Carefully blend the colours to avoid leaving sharp lines. Always consider the direction of the light, and remember that prominent parts of flowers or leaves cast shadows. In working it is best to use several needles, each threaded with a different shade, and join in a new thread by working two small stitches. When using a frame it is difficult to darn in the end of a thread, so finish with a double stitch.

Fig. 30.1c Split stitch on curves.

31 Smocking

Thirteenth-century women and girls wore a loose garment known as a *smoc* or *smicket*, a word derived from the Anglo–Saxon *smoce* meaning a 'garment to creep into'. Later this garment became known as a 'shift' or 'chemise'. These 'smocs' were of fine linen decorated with embroidery, and they gradually changed their appearance although retaining their name.

Smocking is a peasant art that has been carried on in this country for hundreds of years, and up to the beginning of the twentieth century the smock was in general use in many country areas. It was a practical, hardwearing and beautiful garment. The earliest known record of a smock is a picture of the time of Charles I, but it is impossible to see whether the fullness is controlled by stitchery. In the period of Queen Anne, a fair was held annually in Mayfair district, and 'smock races' were held, the prize for the race being a new, embroidered smock. Later, loose garments were worn by shepherds and farm labourers, and these garments became known as smock-frocks. They were made of a strong linen or holland, the bodices and sleeves were elaborately embroidered, and the skirt was loose, hanging straight from the shoulders. As time went on these garments changed, and instead of being straight, they began to have more fullness in the front and back, to give extra room for movement.

There were several different shapes of smocks, varying in different parts of the country, but all were of very simple cut, being entirely based on oblongs and squares, with no curves. Many of them were made simply by folding and cutting. The colour of the smocks too varied in different parts of the country. In many counties a grey or drab was the colour of working smocks. White and natural fabrics were used for those worn around London, and in Hampshire, Berkshire and Wiltshire, while in the Midlands a deep blue smock called a *Newark Frock* was worn. Olive green was commonly found in Essex, Cambridgeshire and Hertfordshire. Black smocks embroidered in white were used in the Isle of Wight and Surrey. Dorset smocks were often embroidered in blue and white, and Sussex was noted for its elaborate smocks which were usually grey or drab worked in white. The Sunday smock was invariably white linen entirely embroidered in white; this seems to have been general throughout the country. In certain places distinctive colours were used for different trades. For example, blue was often the colour of a shepherd's smock.

Before the middle of the eighteenth century smocks were not elaborately decorated, but in the early nineteenth century they reached their greatest perfection. Even then, most of the designs were simple and worked directly onto the fabric without any previous drawing. It is believed that different patterns were used to distinguish the wearers' occupation. In Dorset and possibly in some other counties farmers at 'hirings' inspected men's smocks to tell their craft, emblems of these having been worked on the plain material or 'box' on either side of the 'tubing' or gathering. Emblems were also worked on the collar of the coat-smocks. For example, gardeners had leaves and flowers; shepherds, crooks, hurdles or sheep-pens. Waggoners or carters had cart-wheels, reins, bits, whips and lashes. Milkmaids had butter-pats, churns, and hearts (Fig. 31.1); woodmen, leaves and trees; the grave-digger, crosses. Fig. 31.2 shows a wedding smock embroidered with the traditional designs of Warwickshire shepherds.

The material used for smocks had to be hardwearing. Shakespeare mentioned the 'hempen homespun smock'. The Sunday white smocks were usually of hand-spun and hand-woven linen. Some of the plainer coat-smocks were made of 'drabbette', which was a strong twill material, very stiff, hardwearing and almost waterproof. Strong twisted linen thread was usually used for working the smocking.

The stitches were simple ones such as feather, chain, stem and satin stitch. A great variety of feather stitches were used, especially in Dorset. On the actual gathering or 'tubing', only variations of stem or outline stitches were used. The stitching was amazingly regular and even in tension.

Apart from the smocks made in this country, smocking was used on the national costumes of Hungary, Albania, Russia, and Roumania. It was chiefly used at the neck

Fig. 31.1 Design from the 'box' of a milkmaid's smock from Hertford-shire.

Fig. 31.2 Sampler smock designs (m *M. Newman*). Wedding smock (m *G. Hamilton, GSA*).

Fig. 31.3 Child's cotton dress decorated with smocking to gather the fullness into the yoke. White striped cotton was worked with blue stranded cotton (dm *R. Broughton, ETC*).

and cuffs of blouses. Smocking in Mexico took on a different form from the one with which we are most familiar, though Mexican blouses, too, are cut entirely of straight pieces. Here the fullness is finely gathered, the pattern being made by the running stitches which pick up the gathers. Patterns of birds and animals are formed by missing certain pleats. Thus, the gathering threads will go through most of the pleats but will occasionally remain on the surface to form the required shape. This form of smocking is usually worked with a black thread on a white fabric.

Today, smocking is mainly used on children's clothes, but it can look attractive on blouses or nightdresses. Almost any material can be used, but as the gathering makes for bulk, thinner fabrics are preferable. For children's dresses, cotton, voile, lawn, nylon or silk can be used, while for nightdresses, silk, crêpe-de-chine or nylon is best. Filoselle or stranded cottons can be used for the stitchery, and two or three threads are usually sufficient as the work is better kept dainty.

Smocking is most effective when there is plenty of fullness, and it is best to begin with fabric of three times the required width. Smocking should be worked before the garment is made up. Care in preparing the fabric to be smocked is essential as the whole beauty of the work depends upon the evenness and regularity of the gathers. Transfers of dots are obtainable for smocking, but do not iron them onto delicate fabric. Instead pin the transfer on the wrong side of the fabric, secure the thread firmly at the beginning and take a tacking stitch through each dot, working all the rows of tacking on the wrong side and leaving an end of thread loose at the end of each row. Each row of tacking should be immediately below the previous one. When all the rows are worked, gently tear away the paper transfer. No mark will then be left on the fabric, but the gathers will be evenly placed. Next, draw the threads up, stoke the gathers, then loosen them to within 2 in. of the required width. Tie off the ends of gathering threads in pairs. See that all the gathers lie evenly before beginning to embroider.

The stitchery is worked on the right side, and the gathering threads can be seen between the folds, and can be used as a guide in keeping the smocking straight. There are not many smocking stitches; stem, or outline, cable, honeycomb, and feather are the main ones, and these are worked on the edge of the folds to draw the gathers together. When the smocking is finished, the tacking threads can be removed and the garment made up.

32 Finishing embroidery

Stretching embroidery

When embroidery is finished it should be stretched rather than pressed. Wool work is the only type which should not be stretched. A drawing board and some layers of blotting paper or sheeting are needed. Make a pad of the blotting paper or sheeting and place it flat on the board with the edges parallel to each other. Place the embroidery face downwards on this pad, pin one end to the board keeping the edge of the work parallel to the board. Stretch it evenly, then pin the opposite end of the

Fig. 32.1 Corner of an organdie table-cloth embroidered in pale blue shadow work and with a narrow pin-stitched hem (m *E. Hurst, ETC*).

Fig. 32.2a Decorative edge for organdie.

Fig. 32.2b Eyelet scallops.

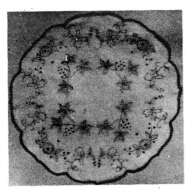

Fig. 32.3 Nylon organza coffee-mat embroidered with eyelets to form a decorative edge (dm *I. Newberry, ETC*).

work, being sure to keep it square. Pins should be about ½ in. apart. Now pin the other sides in the same way. Take a damp sponge and thoroughly moisten the wrong side of the work. Avoid touching the pins with any moisture. Next readjust the pins, pulling the embroidery as tight as possible in each direction. Place a clean piece of paper on top, then a weight, and leave until the fabric is quite dry. If the edge of the embroidery is to show, care needs to be taken to ensure that no rust marks from the pins stain the fabric. This method of stretching will remove any puckers that have come in working, and will give the stitches a raised effect. It is often best to do this before making the outside hem.

Finishes

Every piece of embroidery should be carefully and suitably finished. Finishes appropriate to a particular type of work are dealt with in the relevant chapter, but certain articles and fabrics call for special treatment irrespective of the type of work used on them. The work should always look a whole, and it is best therefore to have in mind right from the beginning how the finished article will appear.

Table-cloths, tray-cloths, table-mats or napkins should be finished according to the fabric used. A linen needs to have a neat hem with mitred corners. When drawn fabric stitches have been used in the embroidery, four-sided stitch is a good way to fix a hem, but for drawn thread-work, hemstitching is better. On an organdie cloth, a very narrow, pinstitched hem will look well (Fig. 32.1). Alternatively the edge can be turned over to form scallops which can be pinstitched. A small coffee cloth or tray-cloth can have a scalloped edge of fine buttonhole stitch, or eyelets can be worked to form a decorative edge

Fig. 32.4 Embroidered tray-cloth (m *Margery Ray, ETC*).

(Fig. 32.2*b* and 32.3). Organdie may also be folded at the edge, then turned down and cut to form triangles of double fabric which are herringboned in place (Figs. 32.2*a* and 32.4).

A narrow binding in a contrasting colour is sometimes effective. This should be a bias strip which is not too wide and clumsy. The toddler's feeder in Fig. 32.5 is bound in scarlet bias to match the scarlet spots of the fabric.

A facing can also be used on linen or organdie. The facing can either form part of the decoration—this is best with transparent fabrics like organdie, or it can be turned to the wrong side where it should be invisibly fastened down or slip-hemmed. A facing can either be on the bias or straight, in cases where there is only one straight side to be neatened.

Hems should be carefully planned so that their width is in proportion to that of the article, and corners should always be mitred (Fig. 32.6). If the hem is not to form part of the decoration, a facing can be used and fastened down on the wrong side. Often however it is preferable to make the hem form part of the decoration, in which case it can be turned to the right side and fastened down with a decorative stitch such as whipped running, blanket, or feather stitch (Fig. 32.7).

Hemstitching is an effective finish to many types of embroidery, especially square or rectangular objects made in linen. First decide how wide the hem is to be, then cut two or three threads and draw them back to make a square hole at each corner. Darn these cut threads a few threads back and cut them off. Turn down the hem and pin it so that it just touches the level of the drawn threads. Next mitre the corners and oversew them with a thread that has been drawn out from the fabric. Tack the hem all around. Hemstitching can then be worked

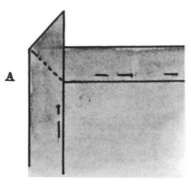

A

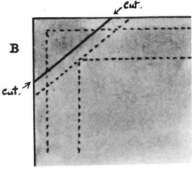

B

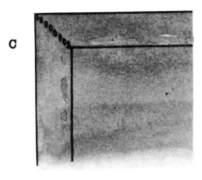

C

Fig. 32.6 *Mitring Corners.*
(*a*) Pin down the hems, then fold the corner over each way to make a diagonal crease.
(*b*) Unfold the corner and cut across, leaving about ⅛ in. turning. Refold the hems turning the ⅛ in. under on the diagonal.
(*c*) Oversew the corner and tack the hems.

Fig. 32.5 Bias binding used to neaten the edge of a toddler's feeder.

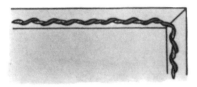

Fig. 32.7a Hem fixed with whipped running stitch.

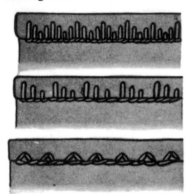

Fig. 32.7b Hem fixed with button-holing.

from left to right on the wrong or right side of the material. Another row of hemstitching may be worked along the opposite edge of the drawn threads. When the same bundle of threads is picked up each side you are using bar or ladder stitch (Fig. 32.8). A zigzag effect can be obtained by picking up in the second row half the threads of the first group, and half the threads of the second group. Even numbers of threads must be grouped together for this type of hemstitching, which is known as serpentine stitch. For other variations of hemstitching see Fig. 16.3.

Antique stitch is another variation of hemstitching. This is worked on the wrong side and is similar to ordinary hemstitching except that the needle should be inserted between the hem and the material, not through both thicknesses. Only small stitches grouping the bundles together can be seen on the right side.

Scalloped edges are effective on cut work, fine linen embroidery or organdie. Two rows of running stitch should be worked along the line of scallops, then button-hole stitch worked over these stitches. The fabric is then cut on the wrong side as close as possible to the knotted edge of the buttonholing (Fig. 32.9). Machine satin stitch can also be used for making a scalloped edge (Fig. 32.10).

Piping is a useful finish for cushions, tea-cosies, or quilted articles. A strip of material one inch wide should be cut on the bias. This should be folded over some piping cord and tacked close to the cord to hold it in position. The piping should next be tacked to the edge of the article on the right side facing inwards towards the centre. The lining material or reverse side is then tacked to this piece, right sides together. Machine stitch around the edge gripping the piping between the two layers of fabric. Turn to the right side and the piping will be in position.

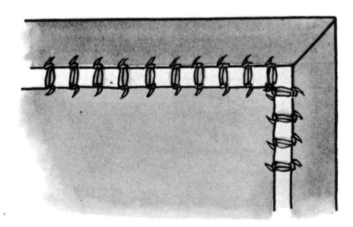

Fig. 32.8 Hem fixed with bar or ladder hemstitching, showing mitred corner.

Fig. 32.11 shows a gingham hot-water bottle cover which is quilted and finished with a piping of bright green as a contrast to the black and white check fabric.

Cushions should be made up so that the cover is easily detachable for washing. Sometimes a zip fastener can be incorporated in the design, to give an attractive opening. Otherwise an opening big enough to insert the cushion should be left and either slipstitched or fastened with press studs once the pad is inside.

The outer edge of a cushion can be neatened with a piping or a decorative cord. A simple twisted, plaited, Greek plaited, finger, knotted or lanyard cord can be used; the threads used in the embroidery should be incorporated in whichever type is chosen.

Simple twisted cord is the easiest cord to make and should usually be made in one or two of the colours that predominate in the embroidery. Three pieces of silk (the same as that used in the embroidery) two and a half times the required length, should be tied together at both ends. Place the loop at one end over a catch or hook, or get someone to hold a pencil through it. Hold the threads taut and with a pencil through the other end begin to turn them, continuing until they are well twisted. Free the loops at each end of the cord, then, holding the middle of the cord with the left hand, double the cord in half so that both ends are held together in the right hand. Release the middle and give the cord a sharp fling in the air. This will allow the cord to twist evenly.

Simple plaited cord. Take four threads and tie them together at one end. Two people, standing side by side, hold the other ends of the threads, one in each hand. One person should then proceed as follows: First, pass the inside thread *under*, and the outside thread *over*, the nearer thread of your partner, both hands thus meeting.

Fig. 32.10 Scalloped edge to an organdie table-mat which was worked on a family sewing machine. Made from the original brush drawing of the horse motif by Mary Kessell (m *Frances Beal; NDS*).

Fig. 32.11 Piping used to finish with contrasting colour a quilted gingham hot-water bottle cover.

Fig. 32.9 Scalloped edge to a table-cloth worked in buttonhole stitch on organdie (m *J. Clements, ETC*).

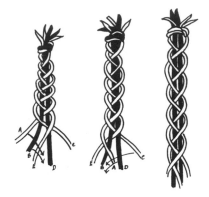

Fig. 32.12a Greek plaited cord.

Fig. 32.12b Finger of knotted cord.

Fig. 32.13 Double finger cord.

Now, making sure that the outside thread crosses over the inside one, change the threads from one hand to the other and sweep the hands back to the original position. Your partner does the same, and you alternate in constant rhythm until the cord is the required length.

Greek plaited cord (Fig. 32.12a) is an attractive flat cord. It is made from five lengths of thread. Two of these (second from either side) form a foundation over which the other three are plaited. Tie the five threads together at one end and secure this end to a catch or hook, and commence plaiting. Bring an outside thread over the next two into the centre. Then (still on the same side) bring the new outside thread (one of the foundations) over the adjacent thread back to its original 'second' position. Repeat these two movements the other side, and continue, alternating each side in turn.

Finger or knotted cord (Figs. 32.12b and 32.14). Tie two thick threads together at one end. Make a loop with one thread, then a loop with the other and put one loop through the other. Pull tight after each loop has been put through the other one. The quickest way of doing this is to hold the knot in the right hand between the thumb and second finger. Loop the thread on the left over the first finger holding the end of this same thread with the third and fourth fingers of the left hand. Next hold the knot with the left hand, leaving go of the loop which has been held by the right first finger and pulling the thread tight. Keep on in this way, changing alternately from left to right hands. Try to make the actions rhythmical.

Double finger cord (Fig. 32.13) is another variation which can be quite effective in two or even four colours. This is different from most plaits, in that two of the threads work from side to side and the other two backwards and forwards. A thick thread is the best material to work with. Knot four lengths together and secure this end. Arrange the four threads in the four directions, cross the two side ones over, then those in front and behind. Continue to cross the threads in the same directions until the cord is completed.

Fringes. Sometimes a fringe on, for example, a stole, or a wall hanging can be an appropriate finish. The simplest fringe can be made by drawing out one thread parallel to the end of the work, about 1 or 1½ in. from its raw edges. Hemstitch, grouping the threads together into bundles of two, three, or four threads. When the hemstitching is completed pull out all the threads from the edge to the stitching line. These threads then form a fringe (Fig. 32.15a). This method was used on the stole in Fig. 17.3. If a deeper fringe is required, hemstitch about 2 or 2½ in. from the edge, draw out all the threads, then knot the groups of threads together (Fig. 32.15b).

A contrasting fringe may be added to a piece of work by using a crochet hook. Cut equal lengths of threads (by winding them round a card), double the length that is required for the finished fringe. Using a fine crochet hook, pull the middle loop of each bundle of threads through the cloth quite near to its edge. The ends of the threads are then passed through the loop and pulled firmly up to the edge of the cloth. Try to tie all the knots evenly (Fig. 32.16a). For a wide fringe the threads may be knotted by taking half the threads from one group and the other half from the next group (Fig. 32.16b).

Tassels can be an effective finish to a bag, a trinket box, or a cushion, or attached to the end of a zip fastener. A tassel should always be round and fat. The easiest one can be made with any embroidery threads. Wind the threads around a piece of card the required length of the

Fig. 32.15a Frayed fringes.

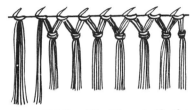

Fig. 32.15b Knotting half the threads from one group and half from the next.

Fig. 32.16a Contrasting fringe.

Fig. 32.16b Knotted fringe.

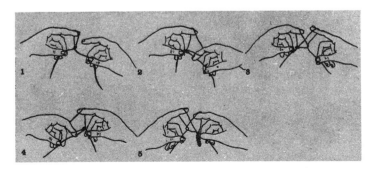

Fig. 32.14 Making a finger cord.

Fig. 32.17a Tassels.

Fig. 32.17b Buttonholed tassel.

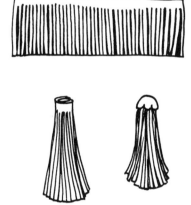

Fig. 32.17c Felt tassel.

tassel (Fig. 32.17a). Cut one end of the threads, remove the card, and tie lightly together at the other end with a piece of thread. The ends can then be frayed and cut level.

Finishing a tassel. The easiest way is to wind thread around the tassel a little distance from the top (Fig. 32.17a). Another method is to work with buttonhole stitch around the threads or cover them with a small piece of felt. Sometimes buttonhole stitch is worked over the top, right down to the binding threads. Each row of buttonholing is worked into the previous one (Fig. 32.17b). Attractive tassels can be made for felt work by cutting strips of felt nearly to the top of the strip. Roll up the strip and stitch it firmly at the top so that it will keep its shape (Fig. 32.17c).

Proportion is most important in making any fringe or tassel. Care needs to be taken that the head of the tassel is not too heavy for the rest of it.

Pompons are sometimes used as a finish to cords on a drawstring bag. These are made by cutting two circles of card of the diameter that is required for the pompon. A small hole is cut in the centre of the cards. Wind a thread which matches the work over the card and through the hole in the middle of it. Continue until the hole is closed. With a pair of sharp, pointed scissors, cut the threads around the circle, between the two layers of card. Next tie a thread tightly around the middle between the cards. Tear away the cards, and the thread which has tied the pompon in the middle can be used to attach it to the work. When finished the pompon can if necessary be trimmed.

A small ball of hard cotton wool can be covered with buttonholing, to make a pompon for the end of a cord. A circle of card covered with fabric to match the work, and decorated with a small embroidered motif can also be used in this way.

Blotters

To make an embroidered cover for a blotter, cut two pieces of card the size required for the finished article, and two pieces $\frac{1}{4}$ in. smaller each way which will be used for the inside. Place the card flat on the embroidered fabric with $\frac{1}{2}$ in. turning of fabric all around. Use a transparent fixative to paste the edges over the card and press flat. The two pieces of card for the inside are covered with fabric in the same way, and the outside and inside pieces stuck together. The back and front of the blotter can be whipped together, and a cord couched over the join.

Trinket boxes

These are made in a similar way (Fig. 32.18). Great accuracy is needed in cutting the pieces of card so that they fit exactly together. The sides, top and bottom can be oversewn into position. Sometimes a layer of cotton wool between the card and the embroidery will soften and improve the lid of a box.

Making up a hanging

After stretching the work cut it to size, leaving one inch turnings. Turn these in and place the work on the lining fabric. Cut out the lining leaving $\frac{1}{4}$ in. turnings. Turn in the lining and tack to the work, taking care that the lining is exactly up to the edge. Oversew the edges together, and afterwards work back over the stitches to form small crosses. The edges can be invisibly slipstitched if desired. When the work has been lined a small row of very tiny, running stitches should be worked about $\frac{3}{4}$ in. from the

Fig. 32.18 Trinket box made from grey and white check gingham, embroidered with scarlet ric-rac and stitchery (dm *Author*).

edge on the wrong side; this will prevent the lining showing over the edges on the right side. Loops of self material can be attached at the top through which a rod may be passed for hanging.

33 Repairing, restoring and cleaning embroidery

Repairs

No two pieces of work are alike and all repairs present their own problems.

In repairing embroidery be very careful to choose the correct colour of thread. For very old work it may be necessary to dip the thread in weak tea or coffee. If it is possible to unravel a thread of the same fabric it will be soft to use, but if this is not possible, a half strand of Filoselle will be suitable. Use a few inches of thread only as it will be easier to pull this gently through the frail fabric.

Broken threads in embroidery can sometimes be fixed with white of egg, which is smoothed on the back with the tip of the finger. Silk embroideries are occasionally repaired by being covered with a fine net of neutral colour to tone with the work. Then with a very fine, bent darning needle (or with a surgical needle) and a very fine silk thread, or a hair, one darns, taking only the smallest stitch on top and catching the net in position. This net will not show at a distance, so this method is sometimes used for repairing church work or regimental colours.

Restoration

With all embroidery it is well to remember the old proverb, 'A stitch in time saves nine'. It is always better to strengthen work when it is becoming weak, and to wash or clean it before it becomes too dirty.

Sometimes it is possible to remount a piece of embroidery on a new ground if the old one has become worn away. The original design should be traced on a stiff open muslin, the design cut out and each part tacked lightly onto the muslin. The whole of this should then be lightly stitched to the new ground. Lines and other small details can be tacked onto the ground through the muslin which will then be cut or pulled away. A piece of backing linen should be mounted on a frame and the new ground mounted on this. Tissue paper can be used instead of muslin for small pieces of work. Outline the design by couching a gold thread or cord.

Cleaning

If you prick your finger and get blood on your work, suck the embroidery immediately and the stain will disappear.

It is unwise to use detergents in embroidery. Linen embroidery worked in fast colours can be safely washed in warm, soapy water. Gently squeeze and rinse thoroughly in several lukewarm waters. Do not wring but roll the work in an absorbent towel, then lay flat on a towel to dry. If you are not sure if the colours are fast, damp a small piece of the back of the work and dry by covering with a clean cloth and pressing with a cool iron. If the colours are not fast they will stain the cloth.

If fragile materials such as silk or satin need cleaning, a little French chalk should be sprinkled on the parts that are dirty. The work is rolled in a clean cloth and left for a few days. After a time the work is shaken well; the dirt disappears with the chalk.

Small spots can sometimes be removed with soap and water; large pieces of work should be sent to a good cleaner.

Fine white work should be washed by being placed in a screw-topped jar of soapy water, and shaken well, or, if it is possible to tack it around a bottle, the latter should be placed in warm soapy water and slowly brought to the boil.

Always press embroidery on the wrong side, first one way, then the other, on a soft pad of clean sheeting.

INDEX